Learning to Laugh

About the author

Gary McGuire has been working in the field of human functioning and strategic life planning for over twenty years. He is a Ph.D. in behavioural science from the University of Minnesota. A professional psychologist, he runs a counseling center in Dallas, Texas.

Learning to Laugh

Gary McGuire

Epitome Books
New Delhi

First published 2009

Published by

Epitome Books

B-65 Mansaram Park
Near Nawada Metro Station
New Delhi – 110 059

Email: info@epitomebooks.com
Web: www.epitomebooks.com

Cataloging in Publication Data–DK
Courtesy: D.K. Agencies (P) Ltd. docinfo@dkagencies.com

McGuire, Gary.
Learning to Laugh / Gary McGuire

p. cm.

Articles on self-development.

ISBN: 978-81-906579-2-1

1. Self-culture. 2. Success. I. Title.

DDC 158.1 22

Printed at Salasar Imaging Systems, Delhi – 35

Preface

There is a role for forced or deliberate laughter. That's because we can still get most of the physiological benefits of hearty laughter regardless of our mood. We don't have to be amused, happy, or have a special occasion to laugh. Merely wanting to improve our well being is good enough reason. With a little practice, we can soon adopt the playful spirit of children who laugh for no other reason than to laugh.

I'm happy to hear you joined a Laughter Yoga class. That is a sign that you refuse to be a victim and choose to take charge of your life. I wish to encourage you to attend the classes and to be patient. The good news is that as long as you do the exercises, you cannot fail. This is because regardless of your mood, your body will benefit from the physiological changes that hearty laughter brings about. Just do your exercises and over time you will begin to feel better. Besides, there's something funny about a roomful of people laughing hysterically without cause, so you may very well end up genuinely laughing and having a great time.

I would like to express my sincere thanks to the publishers for their continued interest in bringing out this book.

Gary McGuire

Contents

1

Learning Self-Discipline

Self-discipline is the mother of happiness

"Self-discipline" makes one think of work or effort, while "happiness" brings up thoughts of pleasure and the absence of work. So, how can the two go together? Well, first we have to understand what happiness is. It is peace of mind. And what exactly does that mean? That simply means FREEDOM FROM shame, guilt, regret, anger, resentment, greed, jealousy, frustration, sadness, self-doubt, fear, boredom, stress, anxiety, loneliness, and all other negative emotions.

Most people sense that happiness and freedom are linked, but only in an imperfect way. For instance, they may think the freedom to stop working and the ability to do anything one pleases will bring happiness. But even if that were the case, the problems of anger, regret, and the other negative feelings would remain. And it is not possible to experience negative emotions and happiness at the same time. Negative feelings are thieves that rob us of happiness.

Here is the paradox: when we seek freedom, we become prisoners, and when we seek self-discipline, we discover freedom. You see, when we seek the freedom to do as we please, we become the prisoners of our emotions. But when we seek the discipline to do what is best for us, we become free to achieve our dreams. Julie Andrews seems to agree, for she said, "Some people regard discipline as a chore. For me, it is a kind of order that sets me free to fly."

Achieving our dreams, by the way, doesn't guarantee our happiness, only freedom from negative emotions does. So, happiness is not about gaining, but about losing. For when we lose, give up, or release our negative feelings, we are, in fact, removing the sludge that covers and has buried the happiness that has always been within us. You see, you were happy as an infant. That is part of your nature; it cannot be removed. But it is often buried under a thick layer of sludge (negative emotions, beliefs, and attitude) which slowly accumulated as you were exposed to more and more toxic experiences.

Well, then, how do we make all the above points practical? How do we apply them to our lives? Let's look at an actual example of a day in the life of Noel Higgins. I don't know about you, but Noel likes to believe that Sunday is a day off from work, a day in which he can do anything he pleases. However, on this particular day, his conscience was reminding him that he should be preparing for a business presentation that he was scheduled to do in a few days. Being Sunday, he didn't feel like working. But he understood it wasn't necessary to enjoy EVERYTHING he did. Enjoy it or not, we need to live up to our obligations. So, Noel packed his bags and headed for the library where he wouldn't be distracted.

Despite not wanting to work, Noel was at the library doing just that. About two and a half hours later, he was growing restless and wondering if he should return home and continue working there. No, he thought, that idea was just a temptation to take a break, so he decided to refocus on the task at hand and get it done as soon as possible. Noel's behavior reminds me of something W. K. Hope said, "Self-discipline is when your conscience tells you to do something and you don't talk back." Noel got the message and didn't talk back. As a result, five hours later, the job was done. Noel left the library with a broad grin on his face. While driving back home, he reflected on what happened. Here's what he discovered:

1. It is within our power to do what we don't want to. It is our responsibility, duty, or obligation that is important, not our feelings.
2. We cannot think of two things at the same time, so once we immerse ourselves in a task, that's all we can think about. All thoughts about whether it is pleasant or not fade from our mind. And as we get involved with the task, it grows increasingly interesting.
3. Thus, the "pain" associated with doing something we don't want to is short-lived. So, real effort is only needed in the beginning. What we need to remember is pain is never permanent. Besides, pain is nothing more than breaking the shell that imprisons us. Our freedom to succeed and get the most from life is worth the effort.
4. After finishing an important task that we didn't feel like doing, there is a feeling of exhilaration. We feel proud of our accomplishment and delighted to learn that we have the self-discipline to take charge of our life. Therefore, what we thought would be painful turns out to be pleasurable.
5. What's more, as we experience this truth, we come to embrace discomfort because of the pleasure conquering it will bring. Not only pleasure, but power. For they who have mastered self-discipline can be, do, or have anything they want. A little effort is a small price to pay for the treasure of success. That's why Leonardo Da Vinci (1452 ~ 1519) rejoiced by saying, "Oh Lord, thou givest us everything, at the price of an effort."

6. When we do what we don't feel like doing because it needs to be done, we develop self-discipline and a strong sense of responsibility, two critical keys to success. As we experience victory after victory, we will grow in confidence, feel exuberant, and know what it truly means to be happy.
7. To avoid missing out on success, we mustn't be tricked into running from responsibility and indulging in some fleeting pleasure. After all, if we were to do so, we will find the "pleasure" (such as watching TV rather than working on an important task) is pleasure in name only. For as we waste valuable time, we will be racked with guilt, greatly diminishing our "pleasure." And whatever momentary pleasure we were to experience, it would only be followed later by stress and regret.
8. When we carefully consider these facts, we will discover that what we usually interpret as pleasurable ends up being painful, and what we first interpret as painful, turns out to be pleasurable. The lesson is, then, we have to think before we act, for the price of living irresponsibly and neglecting our duties is loss of happiness. On the other hand, the result of being self-disciplined and living up to our responsibilities is happiness.

2

Lack of Energy: Have you lost your drive because you're out of gas?

"Help! There's a lot I'd like to do, but I've run out of gas. What can I do?" Lack of energy or exhaustion is a problem that is holding many people back. Energy is the fuel that powers our drive to get things done; constant bouts of exhaustion are the brakes that bring our progress to a halt. So, much is at stake here. Our physical, psychological, and spiritual well-being need high levels of energy. If we wish to reach our potential, it's a subject we must pay attention to. What follows is a glimpse at some of the causes of a lack of energy and some of the methods to develop more energy.

What douses the flames of energy?

Are you wiped out by work? The fatigue that we associate with work often has little to do with it and much to do with a negative attitude. That is, the culprits are not a demanding boss and uncooperative coworkers, but negative emotions. Resentment, impatience, anger, anxiety, envy, fear, and other negative feelings gnaw away at us throughout the day, draining us of all our energy. No wonder we're exhausted. We've got to turn our attitude around. We'll regain much of our lost energy as soon as we start to appreciate what we have, begin to help those around us, and focus on improving ourselves instead of the workplace. Also, it is not the work we do, but the work we don't do that causes exhaustion! In other words, when we do our job, we feel exhilarated, or energetic. But when we procrastinate, we experience guilt, regret, and fear of the future consequences. The result? Stress, or lack of energy.

If you're staying up most of the night partying or hanging out with friends, your body will not have enough time to rejuvenate itself. Lack of sleep is a major cause of fatigue. It's a problem that's easy to fix. Get enough sleep! If it's fun you're looking for, get a life. A life full of energy!

It takes 50% of our energy to digest a meal of fruits, vegetables, grains, and nuts. If our meal consists of cooked and processed foods, our body will direct about 80% of its energy toward digestion. Heavy meals, with fat and sugar, can take up to fourteen hours to digest, forcing your body to work all through the night and early hours of the morning. No wonder you're not full of energy after a night's sleep. So, if you eat more raw fruits and vegetables and less fat and sugar you'll regain some of that lost energy. Overeating is a double attack on the body's limited resources of energy. Not only does it cause the body to work overtime digesting food, but the extra weight that we have to carry throughout the day saps even more energy.

We also need to avoid trying to do too much at one time. By spreading our limited resources of energy over many tasks, none of them receive enough attention, resulting in stress. Far better to do a few things well than many poorly. When we prioritize our tasks and devote our energy on the important matters, we will accomplish more. And those accomplishments will boost our energy.

What fans the flames of energy?

The benefits of working out in the gym, walking to work, or climbing stairs are too numerous to ignore. Exercise creates energy, improves our health, and builds self-discipline and self-esteem. The message is clear: we need to get off our buts and exercise!

All athletes are familiar with the "high" they achieve after strenuous exercise. It allows them to continue past the point of exhaustion. What is true in sports is also true in other areas of life. If we persist in a grueling task, despite the enormous outlay of energy, we will experience a "second wind," and find that we can do even more. William James explains, "If an unusual necessity forces us onward, a surprising thing occurs. The fatigue gets worse up to a certain point, when, gradually or suddenly, it passes away and we are fresher than before! We have evidently tapped a new level of energy. There may be layer after layer of this experience, a third and fourth 'wind.' We find amounts of ease and power that we never dreamed ourselves to own, sources of strength habitually not taxed, because habitually we never push through the obstruction of fatigue."

Good posture and proper breathing are key elements in maximizing energy. Holding the phone with our shoulder and neck instead of our hand, slouching, and poor posture cause muscle strain, draining energy. Also, if we do not sit properly, we do not breathe properly. Shallow, "chest breathing" can reduce our oxygen intake by up to 33%. We need to use our diaphragm when we breathe. That is, our stomach should go out when we inhale and in when we exhale. Proper breathing increases energy.

A deep breathing or meditative exercise is an excellent way to reduce stress and increase energy. Try this exercise: Sit comfortably with eyes closed while maintaining a good posture and fill your lungs with oxygen by inhaling slowly through your nose. Allow the oxygen to travel throughout your body by holding your breath for 4 or 5 seconds. Slowly exhale. Then, hold your breath for 3 or 4 seconds, dissipating stress. Repeat this eight or nine times to complete one set of deep breathing exercises. Three or four sets a day will help to keep your energy level high.

If you're working at a desk most of the day, be sure to get up often and take 15-20-second breaks. Stretch, get the blood flowing, take a deep breath, relish the moment, smile, and get back to work. More than a caffeine break, you need an energy break.

Our body is mostly made of water. We need plenty of it to preserve our energy. Not all liquids are helpful. Coffee and alcohol, for example, are diuretics. That is, they cause you to lose more fluids than you gain. You may want to drink bottled or filtered water, but even plain tap water is better than no water. Many of the problems we experience, such as headaches, are caused by dehydration. So, drink water throughout the day to maintain optimum well-being and energy.

Perhaps the above information, though limited, is enough to get us to re-evaluate our priorities and set out on the road of high-energy living. After all, a life without energy can hardly be called living. Well, pardon me as I leave for a cup of coffee. Whoops, I mean a glass of carrot juice!

3

Lack of Patience: Patience carries a lot of WAIT

One of the great tragedies of life is unfulfilled potential. The world could have had, and should have had, many more police and pilots, engineers and entertainers, composers and chefs, doctors and diplomats, mechanics and masseurs, linguists and librarians, geologists and graphic artists, translators and therapists, nurses and navigators, welders and writers, as well as men and women working in many other occupations. Too often, what could have been, never came about. Although there are many reasons for this, one of the major causes of failure is the inability to persist in the face of seemingly insurmountable difficulties.

If only they had persevered. If only they had refused to give up. If only they had the self-discipline to forge on despite the obstacles that were strewn on the road to success. If only they had the PATIENCE to continue. As we begin a New Year, let's not abandon our dreams and resolutions because of impatience. Rather, let's have the clarity of mind to understand that it takes time for seeds to germinate, plants to grow, and crops to be harvested. Let's also consider the words of Og Mandino (1923 ~ 1996):

"Patience is bitter, but its fruit is sweet. With patience you can bear up under any adversity and survive any defeat. With patience you can control your destiny and have what you will.

Patience is the key to contentment, for you and for those who must live with you. To be brave without patience can kill you. To be ambitious without patience can destroy the most promising of careers. Patience is power. Employ it to stiffen your spirit, sweeten your temper, stifle your anger, bury your envy, subdue your pride, bridle your tongue, restrain your hands, and deliver your whole, in due time, to the life you deserve."

Sometimes the words we use confuse and mislead us. For example, we talk about 'LOSING patience' or not being able to 'FIND the patience' to deal with a situation. Don't get deceived into believing that patience can be lost or found. It is not a commodity. It is a decision. It is a decision to wait. It is a decision to hold on to our dream despite any delays we may have to put up with. Georges-Louis Leclerc Buffon (1707 ~ 1788) was a French Naturalist, so he understood that it takes time for nature to develop her plans. Armed with that insight, he offered this sound advice, "Never think that God's delays are God's denials. Hold on; Hold fast; Hold out. Patience is genius."

Before we leave the subject of 'holding on,' I'd like to share this Pueblo Indian prayer: "Hold on to what is good,/Even if it's a handful of earth.

/Hold on to what you believe,/Even if it's a tree that stands by itself.

/Hold on to what you must do,/Even if it's a long way from here./Hold on to your life,/Even if it's easier to let go./Hold on to my hand, / Even if I've gone away from you."

Patience is not only genius, it is power. Small tasks repeatedly done lead to major accomplishments. Consider the termites of Zambia, for instance. After eating sand, these insects patiently deposit it on the ground, climb onto the deposit and add another layer. Bit by bit, they add layers, until an 'ant hill' is formed that is up to twenty feet tall and fifty feet in diameter! Yet, the stunning achievements of African termites are dwarfed by the incredible potential that lives within YOU. No wonder the Greek poet Hesiod (c. 700 BC) wrote, "If you should put even a little on a little and should do this often, soon this would become big." Another way in which patience is power is in its ability to change the difficult into the easy. Any new task or responsibility is difficult at first. But if we patiently stick to it, it will become easy.

Besides considering what patience is, we should also reflect on what it is not. For example, patience is not despair, indifference, or procrastination. Rather, it is a temporary truce; it is a willingness to accept what cannot be changed NOW. While being patient, we do not remain idle. We change our tactics, look for other solutions, and relentlessly press on. We can never be sure which path will lead us to the goal we desire, so we patiently, persistently, and perseveringly keep trying until we meet with success. Henry Wodsworth Longfellow (1819 ~ 1892) shared his view on the same subject: "Every man must patiently bide his time. He must wait - not in listless idleness but in constant, steady, cheerful endeavors, always willing and fulfilling and accomplishing his task, that when the occasion comes he may be equal to the occasion."

Lack of patience is not a malady. Because it is not an illness, it cannot be used as an excuse. Yet, some will say, "I can't help it. I'm impatient. That's just the way I am!" However, "That's just the way I am!" really means, "That's the way I choose to be." Those who are egocentric, or think they are the center of the universe, make demands on others, and when their unreasonable demands are not met, they become frustrated, irritable, and upset. Such behaviour is not a formula for success. Impatience is a sign of immaturity, and to overcome it we need to start thinking of others and accept responsibility for our personal success.

Patience is a virtue and a key to success. But our patience must be measured and balanced. If it is taken to extremes, we may wait until it is too late. The success, which could have been ours, is lost because of delay. Look at how well this principle is described by the eighteenth century French priest Jacques Roux, "There is a slowness in affairs which ripens them, and a slowness which rots them."

Part of the human experience is coping with illness. When it strikes, our natural reaction may be one of rebellion and rage. However, such feelings are self-destructive and only compound the problem. Trying to cope by gritting our teeth and bearing it isn't much help either because that tactic is undermining. No, the only way to deal with suffering is with patience, for patience prepares us to move on. We willingly accept our lot because we realize it, too, will pass. And if it does not, we have the capacity to accommodate it. If we choose to, we can muster up sufficient strength to accept the challenge of the Greek philosopher, Epictetus (55 ~ 135 AD), who said, "Dare to look up to God and say, 'Deal with me in the future as Thou wilt; I am of the same mind as Thou art; I am Thine; I refuse nothing that pleases Thee; lead me where Thou wilt; clothe me in any dress Thou choosest.'"

4

Law of Compensation

There is no dispensation from the Law of Compensation

In modern terms, we could say one man is rich but bored and another is poor, yet happy. One woman achieves great success but dies young; another is less successful but lives longer. Or, a rich man can afford steak and lobster but finds it hard to digest while a poor man has a hearty appetite and good health. Or, someone else may have a large salary, but little time to spend with their family.

Ralph Waldo Emerson (1803 ~ 1882) explains compensation in clear terms: "For everything you have missed, you have gained something else; and for everything you gain, you lose something else." Again, in his journal dated January 8, 1826, he writes, "The whole of what we know is a system of compensations. Every defect in one manner is made up in another. Every suffering is rewarded; every sacrifice is made up; every debt is paid."

The title of this article, then, means there is no exemption, no exception, or no escape from this law of life. We cannot have successes without failures or hardships without gains. For every gain, there is a loss. We lose the wood to gain fire and heat. We lose the heat to cook the food. We lose the food to nourish our body, and so it goes. This law of nature is about balance, harmony, and equilibrium. It is similar to the Law of Conservation of Energy in science. (Energy may neither be created nor destroyed and the sum of all energy remains constant.)

Another aspect of the Law of Compensation is that we will reap what we sow. Isn't it true that if I plant tomatoes, I'll reap tomatoes, and if I plant weeds, I'll reap weeds? So, it should come as no surprise that if I plant seeds of love, I will be loved, and if I plant acts of kindness, others will treat me kindly. But if all I sow is anger, all I reap will be hostility. When we practice the Golden Rule by treating our neighbors as we wish to be treated, we live in harmony with this principle and will reap its benefits. Or, as Ralph Waldo Emerson put it, "It is one of the most beautiful compensations in life that no man can sincerely try to help another without helping himself."

Another term to describe reaping what we sow is 'karma.' In Sanskrit, karma means action or deed. In the spiritual sense, it means both our actions and the consequences that flow from them. Those who believe in karma believe that their fate is governed by the choices they make. The happiness they experience or the suffering they undergo is a result of how they use their free will. So, it's just another way to describe how we reap what we sow.

Yet another term used to describe the same thing is The Law of Action and Reaction. That is, for every force, there is a counter force. The greater we stretch a rubber band, the greater its snapback. The more I scowl at you, the angrier you will the more you smile at me, the more pleased I will. We could also express this idea by calling it the Law of Cause and Effect, or just by saying that virtue is its own reward and wrongdoing causes suffering.

The Law of Compensation, or sowing what we reap, is not about God punishing the wicked and rewarding the holy, but simply His law of natural consequences. If we fall into a fire, we are burned not because we're evil, but because of the heat of the flames. So, it is wise to become familiar with the laws of nature to avoid unnecessary pain and unhappiness.

Once we understand for every gain there is a loss, we can free ourselves from envy and live contentedly. Blessed are the contented, for they are never poor. Woe unto the discontented, for they are never rich. Blessed is she who has little and wants less, for she is richer than he who has much and wants more. Blessed, too, is he who realizes that a little is a great deal when it is enough. And, as Socrates (469 ~ 399 BC) taught, "He is the richest who is content with the least."

There is a time for contentment and a time for discontentment. When we use discontent to raise ourselves to a higher level, we are living in line with the Law of Compensation. For at such a time, we realize that there is no gain without loss, or no gain without pain. We understand that our success depends not on what we take up, but what we give up. So, we willingly sacrifice time and comfort to reach our goal. And if we experience a temporary setback, we're not discouraged because we understand that hidden in our problems are blessings waiting to be discovered. In the same way, when we are pounded by adversity, we find solace in the Law of Compensation, looking forward to the benefits that await us.

Also, we don't make the mistake of comparing our lives with those of others. For although their gains are clearly visible, their loses are hidden from view. Neither do we allow our imagination to exaggerate the extent of our losses or others' gains. We also keep our balance by remembering that all is relative. After all, bad is never good, until worse happens.

5

Laziness at Work

The lazy rest without comfort and sleep without peace of mind.

We can always love anything we do, and do it at any time and at any place. Once we awaken to this fact, we will no longer need to move from place to place or job to job. What we often forget is that love is a choice. It doesn't matter if the object of our love is a person, place, thing, idea, or job; love is something we choose to give away. Interestingly, the more we give away, the more it flows right back into our lives. Since we always have the energy to do what we love, the solution to your problem is to learn to love whatever needs to be done to improve our life.

So, why don't you love your job? Well, this leads to secret number two: Your lack of interest in your job (and resultant lack of energy) has nothing to do with the contents of your job and everything to do with the contents of your mind. You haven't yet learned how to focus on the right things. When it comes to your job, all you can think about are unpleasant things. You do this automatically, without making a conscious choice.

Love is based on knowledge. If you can't think of anything positive about your job, how can you love it? In your case, you probably are not entirely negative, but appreciating one or two of the hundreds (yes, hundreds!) of positive things about your job isn't good enough. Realize, the tools we use to create our lives are our predominant thoughts. In other words, if most of our thoughts are negative, we will lead negative lives. In summary, whether you say you love your job or whether you say you hate it, you are right because thoughts are self-fulfilling prophecies. In other words, your thoughts make it so.

So, to break the cycle of negativity, you have to get into the habit of counting your blessings instead of counting your so-called misfortunes.

Start today by making a list entitled "What I like about my job." And keep adding to the list every day. As the days pass, the message will slowly sink in and you will realize how fortunate you are. Your problem was simply a matter of forgetting to look for the good, but you can start remedying that today.

Don't worry about cheating your employers, they became successful before you entered the picture and remained successful after you left. No, the person you need to worry about cheating is yourself. Don't rob yourself of opportunities, pride, satisfaction, confidence, self-respect, self-esteem, peace of mind, happiness, and a good night's sleep.

Speaking in terms you readily understand, remember that you are the author, producer, and director of your life. If you are unhappy with the present situation, change the script. How should you change it? Well, make the hero of your play (life) a woman committed to being the best secretary possible. See her welcome every challenge as an opportunity to develop self-discipline, gain new skills, and grow increasingly powerful. See her life become filled with purpose.

In your script, make her more concerned about the problems of her boss and coworkers than about her own. In other words, don't let the hero see herself as burdened with tasks. Rather, let her see herself as lightening the burdens of her boss and coworkers. Let her see her work as worthwhile and watch her grow in esteem and self-esteem.

Make the star of your play playful. So, even when swamped with unpleasant tasks, make her play a game of "How many hateful tasks can I get done today?" Let her keep score and watch her grow in confidence and cheerfulness. Use your creative talent to create your own joyous life.

You have arrived where you are today because of your choices. If you are unhappy about your present circumstances, that simply means you'll have to change the way you choose to act. To learn how, go to the library and get this must-read: *CHOICES: Manage Your Choices and You Will Manage Your Life,* by Shad Helmstetter (any book written by him is worth reading), Pocket Books, 1990.

For a change of attitude, read *ATTITUDE IS EVERYTHING: 10 Life-Changing Steps to Turning Attitude into Action,* Keith Harrell, HarperBusiness Paperback, 2003. If you read this book, be sure to also get the workbook: *THE ATTITUDE IS EVERYTHING WORKBOOK: Strategies and Tools for Developing Personal and Professional Success,* Keith Harrell, HarperCollins, 2003.

To learn how to overcome regrets, mistakes, and missed opportunities, read: *Woulda, Coulda, Shoulda,* by Dr. Arthur Freeman and Rose DeWolf, Silver Arrow Books, William Morrow, 1989.

To overcome self-defeating behavior, read: *Self-Defeating Behaviors,* by Milton R. Cudney, Ph.D. and Robert E. Hardy, Ed.D., HarperSanFrancisco, 1991.

Yes, you can change at any age. Start by thinking about the subject seriously. As the venerable Khenchen Konchog Gyaltshen Rinpoche wrote, "If our clothes are caught on fire, would we just stay there and let them burn?"

Similarly, when laziness comes, we should always try to overcome it. If a snake comes on your lap, how quickly you will stand up and shout!

Similarly, when laziness comes, act like that."

We become a better person by improving the world. And we improve the world by shifting our focus away from our problems to the problems of others. We make this a better world when we ask and act on questions like, "How can I help my boss, coworkers, neighbors, family, friends, and those in need?"

6

Learn From Children

A torn jacket is soon mended; but hard words bruise the heart of a child. (Longfellow)

"Children today are tyrants. They contradict their parents, gobble their food, and tyrannize their teachers." Sounds familiar? Who do you suppose said that? It was Socrates! He said that more than 2,400 years ago. So the world hasn't changed much, has it? It seems middle-aged people feel threatened by youngsters. They don't like their rude behavior and the way they dress. What has changed, however, is not the behavior of children, but our own memory.

Just in case you forgot, here's Viola Spolin to refresh your memory: "We forget what it's like to be a child. There are few places outside his own play where a child can contribute to the world in which he finds himself. His world: dominated by adults who tell him what to do and when to do it - benevolent tyrants who dispense gifts to their "good" subjects and punishment to their "bad" ones, who are amused at the "cleverness" of children and annoyed by their "stupidities."

True, there is youth crime and violence, but isn't this a case of children doing to society what was done to them? Where do you suppose most abandoned children live? At home! Though they live at home, many children are ignored by their parents. Perhaps kids run away from home because they're looking for their parents. When children are deprived of love, why are we surprised that they turn out bad? There's something wrong when the TV set is better adjusted than our kids, but whose fault is that? The truth is children are a godsend. We can learn from them. That's why Christ said, "Truly, I say to you, unless you turn and become like children, you will never enter the kingdom of heaven." (Matthew 18:3).

What we learn from children

Children are pure. They are innocent. See how they play with their neighbors. Race, ethnicity, religion, gender are foreign to them. Everyone is valued as a friend and all are treated equally (until adults interfere and teach them prejudice).

Children are honest. They speak from their hearts. Adults wear masks, hiding their thoughts. They are afraid to speak the truth, afraid to expose their true selves. Not so for children, for they have courage. John Bradshaw explains, "Children are curious and are risk takers. They have lots of courage. They venture out into a world that is immense and dangerous. A child initially trusts life and the processes of life."

Children can make us more spiritual. They are bubbling over with happiness and unconditional love. To become like children is to love the world unconditionally. We create children, but they create spiritual beings by teaching us the power of love. Also, learn from children the joy of simple pleasures. To a three-year-old child, a green caterpillar can be more exciting than a $300 seesaw.

How to rear children

Your primary responsibility to your children is to guard their happiness and return their love. They don't need your presents; they need your presence. Mark Twain explains: "We are always too busy for our children; we never give them the time or interest they deserve. We lavish gifts upon them; but the most precious gift -our personal association, which means so much to them - we give grudgingly."

Read how Midge Decter apologizes to children on our behalf: "It might sound a paradoxical thing to say - for surely never has a generation of children occupied more sheer hours of parental time --but the truth is that we neglected you. We allowed you a charade of trivial freedoms in order to avoid making those impositions on you that are in the end both the training ground and proving ground for true independence. We pronounced you strong when you were still weak in order to avoid the struggles with you that would have fed your true strength. We proclaimed you sound when you were foolish in order to avoid taking part in the long, slow, slogging effort that is the only route to genuine maturity of mind and feeling. Thus, it was no small anomaly of your growing up that while you were the most indulged generation, you were also in many ways the most abandoned to your own meager devices by those into whose safe-keeping you had been given."

How can children learn how to live right if they've never seen it done? They need models, not critics. They will follow our example, not our advice. So, how shall we teach them? By example!

Parents are often heard saying, "Pay attention when I speak." But why don't we pay attention when they speak? The smallest event in your child's life is an event in their world. It is, therefore, a world event. To your child it is significant; pay attention to it.

Your children are in critical need of nurturing. They need your encouragement, praise, and support. They need a willing ear to hear their concerns and a tight hug that expresses your unconditional acceptance and total commitment. Don't worry about what they will be tomorrow, but focus on what they are today. The best way to bring up children is never to let them down. Here's another tip that comes from Lady Bird Johnson, "Believe in them; children are apt to live up to what you believe of them."

We also need to teach our children responsibility. As Ann Landers wrote, "What the vast majority of American children needs is to stop being pampered, stop being indulged, stop being chauffeured, stop being catered to. In the final analysis it is not what you do for your children but what you have taught them to do for themselves that will make them successful human beings."

When you were a youngster, your mom quickly mended your torn jacket. But when the harsh words of your parents bruised your heart, how many years did it take for your heart to heal? Perhaps it still hurts. Your parents meant well. They didn't know better, so forgive them. But learn from their mistakes and avoid bruising the hearts of your children.

7

Learning Patience

Lord, grant me patience, and do it NOW!

Patience is the ability to wait for the fruition of our goals. Or, as the ancient philosopher Epictetus is reported to have said nearly 2,000 years ago, "Nothing great is created suddenly, any more than a bunch of grapes or a fig. If you tell me that you desire a fig. I answer you that there must be time. Let it first blossom, then bear fruit, then ripen." It takes time to do worthwhile things, so those who lack the patience to persist will fail to accomplish much. Do we want to develop as much of our potential as possible? If so, we'll have to learn how to be patient.

Being patient doesn't mean sitting around waiting for things to happen. Instead, it means to work as hard and as long as necessary, without giving up, until we reach our destination. The ancient Egyptians didn't sit around waiting. They made plans, preparations, and worked on their project until the pyramids were completed. The pyramids, then, are monuments to patience. They are a reminder that if we persist in our personal projects while enduring the necessary wait, we will finally succeed. After getting their fill of mulberry leaves, silkworms make silk cocoons, which the Chinese and Japanese used to weave silk gowns and kimonos. That explains the Chinese proverb, "With time and patience the mulberry leaf becomes a silk gown." Clearly, patience is power.

Patience is not only about enduring a long wait, it is also about enduring insults, provocation, and mistreatment without resentment, anger, or bitterness. Why put up with abuse? Because patience is also an expression of compassion. Because we are compassionate, we tolerate the faults of others. Because we are strong and they are weak, we accept their abuse with a smile and wish them well.

Buddhists commonly refer to patience as armor that protects the compassionate person from the barbs and verbal attacks of others. Interestingly, Leonardo Da Vinci had a similar idea, for he wrote, "Patience serves as a protection against wrongs as clothes do against cold. For if you put on more clothes as the cold increases, it will have no power to hurt you. So in like manner you must grow in patience when you meet with great wrongs, and they will be powerless to vex your mind."

Almost all violence stems from anger, and patience often has the power to neutralize it. So, patience is a tool of the peacemaker. To eliminate possible misunderstanding, let me give one example of patiently accepting abuse and then contrast it with an example in which impatience is warranted.

In the first example, let's say my supervisor at work always treats me condescendingly. Regardless how hard I work, he treats me without respect. Yet, I patiently bear his abuse. Why? Because I recognize he is a fellow human being. A human being with pain. Perhaps he feels threatened by my performance. Perhaps the source of his cruel remarks is fear. In other words, his abuse exposes him as the weakling he is. Instead of kicking a weak person by fighting back, shouldn't I be compassionate? After all, if I bear my abuser's cruelty with a smile, he may eventually learn that I am not a threat. If so, instead of upsetting him, I would have uplifted him. And by doing so, I would have made the world a better place.

However, at times, impatience is called for. For example, we must not tolerate child abuse or wife beating. Also, anything greater than zero tolerance of violence must not be permitted in our schools. Although abusers are sick and in need of help, our compassion is first directed toward their victims, who are in immediate need of help. After the victims are rescued, we can try to rehabilitate the abuser.

A society based on consumerism boosts profits by preaching the doctrine of impatience. "Don't wait; act now! Don't wait until you can afford it; buy it now with a credit card! Why prepare for your future by working hard for many years when you can strike it rich NOW by winning the lottery or a casino jackpot?" Patience is out of the window and instant gratification is banging on our door. When we abandon patience, we abandon self-discipline. A world without either is a world without Mozart, Thomas Edison, or Tiger Woods. It is also a world without Olympic Gold Medal winners, astronauts, professors, corner pharmacists, auto mechanics and countless other members of industry, trade, and the arts. Can you think of anything worthwhile that can be achieved without giving up immediate gratification for long-term gain?

In a single day we can be faced with countless irritations: someone tailgates you on your way to work; someone cuts in front of you while you're waiting in line at the post office; coworkers chat and laugh loudly in the next cubicle while you're conducting a business phone call; you're going out with friends tonight, but they show up an hour late, or you're cooking dinner when you're suddenly interrupted by a telemarketer. I'm sure you can think of many other examples. So, what do we do when we encounter an endless stream of minor irritants? Well, we can choose to become upset or we can choose to follow the example of oysters. They use an irritating grain of sand to create a glittering pearl. We can use our irritating experiences to create pearls of forgiveness, pearls of compassion, and pearls of understanding.

Learning to accept minor irritations prepares us to endure major ones. Those who lack patience find minor irritations or suffering unbearable. However, those who have mastered patience find great suffering tolerable. Patience has great impact on our happiness, for how can those who are upset and constantly complain be happy? Those who are always angry withdraw from the world; they curse the world. But those who are patient are peacemakers who embrace the world, bless it, and thank it for the opportunity to create pearls.

How can we expect to have others accept our weaknesses unless we are willing to accept theirs? Patience, then, is about respect for others. It is when we interact with others that we come to understand ourselves. For when we act with patience and understanding, that's what we become. And when we act with impatience and anger, that's what we are.

How can we commit to a relationship unless we have patience? Patience binds, heals, and supports relationships. Impatience is divisive. It severs friendships, dissolves marriages, breaks up families, and breaks hearts. So, patience is also about maturity. Patient people do not throw away pets and possessions or relationships and responsibilities simply because things aren't working out as originally expected. Patient people bring out the best in them. Impatient people bring out the beast in them.

You say you're not as patient as you would like to be? Not to worry, just be patient, for patience comes to those who wait. Aren't all things difficult before they become easy? My final words on patience are taken from the eighteenth-century French naturalist, Georges-Louis Leclerc Buffon (1707-1788), "The ability to accept delay. Or disappointment. To smile at setbacks and respond with a pleasant, understanding spirit. To remain calm while others around are uneasy. This is Godly patience. Never think that God's delays are God's denials. Hold on; Hold fast; Hold out. Patience is genius."

8

Learning to Compromise

Don't agonize, compromise

People: we can't get along without them and we can't get along with them. We can't get along without them because we can't do everything; we need their help, and they need ours. We can't get along with them because their interests and goals clash with ours. So, how do we reconcile these differences? How do we change frustration, bickering, and interference into cooperation? The answer is with compromise.

Compromise is a pillar of society, for it restores harmony, overcomes distrust and suspicion, and leads to cooperation. Edmund Burke (1729 ~ 1797) puts it this way, "All government, - indeed, every human benefit and enjoyment, every virtue and every prudent act, - is founded on compromise and barter." It is helpful to remember that EVERYTHING IS FOUNDED ON COMPROMISE. Think about it. Your job is a compromise between salary and responsibility; the car you drive, between performance and efficiency; the products you buy, between quality and low price; the medicine you may take, between benefits and side effects, and your marriage, between give and take.

Our first act must be one of compromise, conciliation, reconciliation, accommodation, give and take, and concession. Don't even bother worshipping God until you have done so. For Christ has taught, ""If you are offering your gift at the altar, and there remember that your brother has something against you, leave your gift there before the altar and go: first be reconciled to your brother, and then come, and offer your gift." (Matthew 5:24) As long as we keep the need for compromise foremost in our minds, we'll have a trouble-free life.

The wise realize that it is better to bend than to break, and better to give a little than to receive nothing. Yes, it is in our self-interest to make concessions and accommodate others. But as we grow more aware, we come to understand that compromising is not only about offering concessions; it is also about offering respect and a willingness to help. Compromise, then, becomes an opportunity to bring happiness to others. Even after giving away a bouquet of flowers, their fragrance lingers in our clothing, and even after leaving someone we have helped, their happiness lingers in our mind. So, you see, compromising is not about agonizing, but about success, harmony, and happiness.

Daily, innocent men, women, and children are needlessly killed in the crossfire of warring parties. Can there be peace without accommodation, reconciliation, and compromise? Some of the obstacles to peace are the scriptures followed by those at war. For example, is the following passage a road map to peace? "When Yahweh your gods has settled you in the land you're about to occupy, and driven out many infidels before you... you're to cut them down and exterminate them. You're to make no compromise with them or show them any mercy." (Deut. 7:1)

The scriptures of other religions are just as harmful. As long as religious leaders and their followers insist that every word of scripture is the word of God, they will be able to justify their barbaric butchery. But, scriptures contain venom as well as wisdom, love as well as hatred, treachery as well as brotherhood, and deceit as well as sacrifice. Until we recognize there are both good and bad in the scriptures that have been handed down to us, we will be unable to choose the good and dismiss the bad. It is time to do some pruning, time to uproot the weeds that are choking all prospects for peace, and time to replace vengeance with reconciliation.

Instead of filling mortuaries with bodies and hospitals with wounded, we need to fill towns and villages with jobs and opportunities. Rather than waging war with 'terrorists,' we need to wage war with poverty. Instead of smiting our enemy with a sword, we need to offer a helping hand. Instead of trampling our enemy beneath our boots, we need to uplift him with respect and hope. There is nothing wrong with destroying our enemy, as long as we do so by making him our friend.

Compromise isn't always a worthy goal. If some friends tell a teen to join them in stealing a car to go out for a 'joyride,' he shouldn't compromise his principles. He shouldn't compromise his integrity. Sometimes it takes courage to do the right thing, but by refusing to become a thief, he protects his friends and society from loss of property.

Another factor to consider is our motivation. When we compromise out of fear, it is not a compromise, but submission; it is not a compromise, but appeasement. We don't help the world by giving in to bullies; on the contrary, doing so empowers them and encourages them to intimidate and manipulate others.

Compromise is about mutual respect and mutual support. Beware of those who take advantage of others by taking without giving anything in return. They like to manipulate others by making them feel guilty. For example, perhaps a coworker regularly blows his money and comes to you whining, "Oh, I ran out of money again and I'm s-o-o hungry! Can you buy me lunch (again)?" It is not helpful to give in because to do so would encourage the manipulator to remain dependent on others, instead of learning the consequences of his actions. Besides, helping the undeserving may deprive you of the means to help someone more deserving.

Don't make it your goal to be liked by everyone. For to do so will tempt you to give in to the demands of others. Instead, make it your goal to do the right thing. Compromising is a necessary and good thing, except when it is a bad thing. At such a time, don't do it. At times, we fail to do the right thing because of fear. To lessen that likelihood, consider the following words of Marianne Williamson, which are taken from her book "*A Return to Love: Reflections on the Principles of A Course in Miracles* (Harper Collins, 1992, chapter 7, section 3). Before sharing her poem, I'd like to mention that Nelson Mandela was so moved by it that he quoted it in his 1994 inaugural speech. Here is Marianne Williamson's "Our Deepest Fear."

Our deepest fear is not that we are inadequate -

our deepest fear is that

we are powerful beyond measure.

It is our light, not our darkness, that most frightens us.

We ask ourselves, "Who am I to be

brilliant, gorgeous, talented, fabulous?"

Actually, who are you not to be?

You are a child of God.

Your playing small doesn't serve the world.

There's nothing enlightened about shrinking

so that other people won't feel insecure around you.

We are born to make manifest

the Glory of God that is within us.
It's not just in some of us; it's in everyone.
And as we let our light shine, we unconsciously
give other people permission to do the same.
As we are liberated from our own fear,
our presence automatically liberates others.

9

Learning to Laugh

I live to laugh and laugh to live

There is a role for forced or deliberate laughter. That's because we can still get most of the physiological benefits of hearty laughter regardless of our mood. We don't have to be amused, happy, or have a special occasion to laugh. Merely wanting to improve our well being is good enough reason. With a little practice, we can soon adopt the playful spirit of children who laugh for no other reason than to laugh.

I'm happy to hear you joined a Laughter Yoga class. That is a sign that you refuse to be a victim and choose to take charge of your life. I wish to encourage you to attend the classes and to be patient. The good news is that as long as you do the exercises, you cannot fail. This is because regardless of your mood, your body will benefit from the physiological changes that hearty laughter brings about. Just do your exercises and over time you will begin to feel better. Besides, there's something funny about a roomful of people laughing hysterically without cause, so you may very well end up genuinely laughing and having a great time.

Thanks to the efforts of Dr. Madan Kataria (a doctor from Mumbai, India), there are now 5,000 (Yoga) Laughter Clubs around the world, with at least a quarter million members belly laughing and enjoying good health. Because of the benefits of laughter, consider joining or forming your own Laughter Club.

Here are more considerations that may apply to our reader's question.

1. If you are suffering from General Anxiety Disorder (GAD) or Clinical Depression, be sure to get the professional help you need. For you won't be able to laugh until you free yourself from obsessive worry and lift your mood.
2. Workplace burnout is another major cause for losing one's ability to laugh. If that describes you, a change in lifestyle is called for. That is, you need more balance, time for play and relaxation as well as work. It's hard to laugh when you don't have time for mirth.
3. Experiencing a trauma is like being badly wounded. Trauma victims need to be healed before they can laugh again. One of the most serious traumas is the loss of a loved one.
4. Yet another reason for the absence of laughter in one's life is the inability to laugh at oneself and accept criticism. If we are overly sensitive, we will be too tense for laughter. Remember the natural habitat of laughter is relaxation. So stop worrying about what others are thinking about you because they're not. That's right, they're not thinking about you because they're too busy worrying about themselves. So, relax!
5. Develop your sense of humor. A sense of humor is the ability to see and laugh at the incongruities of life. For example, imagine a disabled man with a sense of humor struggling to row a canoe in a pond. He's moving so slowly that a turtle passes him! "I lost a race to a turtle!" laughs the man. Become like him, ever watchful and aware of the inconsistencies and absurdities of life so you will always have something to laugh about, regardless of the severity of the challenges you face.

6. Hang out with children. You'll soon be taken in by their innocence and playfulness. Forget about yourself; brighten up their day by making them laugh, and you soon will be laughing too.
7. Until you relearn the art of laughing, practice smiling. Like Laughter Yoga, you don't need a reason to do it; just do it and experience the benefits. Psychologist Paul Ekman (Human Interaction Lab at the University of California in San Francisco) says real and fake smiles have the same positive effects on brain activity, skin temperature, heart rate and respiration.
8. Use the Internet as a source of funny photos, cartoons, and jokes. Make your own humor scrapbook. Just ten minutes a day spent on studying humor will pay big dividends in the future. Be patient and remember not to force anything. Just relax and eventually laughter will happen to you.
9. Heed this advice from Og Mandino (1923 ~1996), "Laugh at yourself and at life. Not in the spirit of derision or whining self-pity, but as a remedy, a miracle drug, that will ease your pain, cure your depression, and help you to put in perspective that seemingly terrible defeat and worry with laughter at your predicaments, thus freeing your mind to think clearly toward the solution that is certain to come. Never take yourself too seriously."

Finally, here's what a sacred scripture has to say on the subject, "A merry heart doeth good like a medicine: but a broken spirit drieth the bones." (Proverbs 17:22, KJV), or for a more modern version of the same verse, "A cheerful disposition is good for your health; gloom and doom leave you bone-tired." (MSG). But what do you do if you don't have a merry heart or cheerful disposition? The answer is LAUGH. After all, as William James (1842 ~ 1910) said, "We don't laugh because we're happy -- we're happy because we laugh."

10

Let go of Spite

Letting go of spite, in spite of ourselves

Were you ever driving along on the highway when someone behind you flashed their high beams because they wanted you to speed up? Such rude and unwarranted behavior can be upsetting. Did you deliberately slow down instead, just to annoy the car behind you? If you did, the other driver just got angrier and probably started tailgating you.

Why do we allow trivial things to upset us? When someone offends us, why do we have to strike back or get even? Why do we retaliate, seek vengeance, or act vindictively? Do we really think being spiteful will improve the situation? If someone flashes their high beams on me, I can either get out of their way or I can contribute to road rage. Why should I become another lunatic driver when there are already too many on the road?

If I'm bothered by the high beams, all I have to do is change lanes and allow the driver behind me to pass. Isn't that simple enough? For many it is not. After all, they were reared in a society that preaches, "Don't get mad! Get even!" None of this "turn the other cheek" or "forgive and let live" for them. No way. They don't want people walking all over them. They don't want to be meek or weak. They demand respect, and if they don't get it, they'll fight for it.

But what if the driver behind you was your brother or sister? Wouldn't you want to be more forgiving? Well, who do you think the other driver is? We're all brothers and sisters, you know. Brothers and sisters with faults. If we can accept that, we'll be able to get along a lot easier.

The problem is many people don't use their brains to think instead they use their heart to feel. They're not logical or rational. They're emotional. So, when someone treats them abrasively, they strike back by making snide remarks, complaining, pouting, and spreading gossip. Or, they may choose to belittle, criticize, ridicule, and humiliate their "opponent." Even those who are supposed to be in love, husbands and wives, may substitute warm hugs for cold shoulders and the silent treatment.

Why do we act so spiteful whenever we think we're being treated unfairly? There are several reasons. First, our sense of justice. If someone causes us pain, we feel it is pay back time. Time to make them suffer. But what if the party that offended us acted inappropriately because they were thoughtless, careless, or just plain stupid? What kind of justice is it that strikes back on the weak?

Another reason is based on the distorted logic that if I make them feel the pain I experienced, they will feel remorseful and apologize. If we were to think with our brain instead of our emotions, we would realize that striking back doesn't solve the problem, it only escalates it. Tit-for-tat, an eye for an eye never works. Ask the Israelis and Palestinians, they know all about it.

Perhaps the biggest reason for refusing to forgive those who offend us is because blaming them for our pain allows us to escape the responsibility of looking after our own happiness. Once we take responsibility, we'll be able to shed the limiting beliefs and negative behavior that blocks our loving nature and natural happiness.

So, how do we take responsibility? Begin by growing in awareness. Understand the nature of life and humanity. Realize the pain you feel is not caused by the actions of others, but by your reactions to their behavior. Why are people so mean to you? Because they are in pain; they are insecure; they feel threatened by you; they are immature and weak. Once you fully understand this, you will respond to their cry for help with compassion instead of anger. You will act with kindness instead of spite. As you grow in understanding, you will be able to place yourself in their shoes and discover why they feel as they do. And after doing so, you will be able to offer them comfort by accepting them, respecting them, and guiding them by your example. By doing so, you will ennoble yourself and others.

Another way of taking responsibility for our own happiness is by letting go of resentment, anger, and spite. We do this by forgiving those we believe have offended us. If you're still harboring ill feelings toward others, it's time to let go. For as Confucius taught, "To be wronged is nothing, unless you continue to remember it." Instead of focusing on how you have been wronged, focus on how you will ennoble yourself and unfold your extraordinary potential. Heal yourself with the balm of forgiveness and allow it to soothe your soul.

Take responsibility for your own happiness by embracing humility. Don't become ensnared in feelings of self-importance. Ironically, it is only by being humble that we add value or importance to the world. For those who are proud are easily offended. They are quick to become outraged by the actions of others. But those who are humble and forgive all, discover happiness. Remember, as Robin Casarjian writes, "Forgiveness restores our hearts to the innocence that we knew - an innocence that allowed us the freedom to love."

Practicing the principles already discussed leads to self-empowerment, growth, and strength. You will discover that when others shoot you with bullets of insults, contempt, and abuse, they are shooting blanks. For when you are loving, accepting, and forgiving, who is there to fear? Who is there to be threatened by? You will be secure in your own love and unharmed by the attacks of others. Each affront that we face is an opportunity to become MORE than what we are, so welcome the barbs thrown your way and dissolve them with your love.

When we abandon retaliation and embrace understanding, we create a better world for ourselves and our children. We will also free ourselves from regrets, guilt, and self-inflicted pain. Seeing everyone as our brother or sister is more than an act of ennoblement, it is a shift in consciousness, a clearer awareness of the web of life.

Instead of acting OUT of spite, we can act IN spite. That is, we can act in spite of our anger, pain, embarrassment, or humiliation - we can act with forgiveness. In spite of ourselves, we can let go of spite and create a better world. I'll close with the words of the former British Prime Minister, Arthur James Balfour (1848-1930), "The best thing to give to your enemy is forgiveness; to an opponent, tolerance; to a friend, your heart; to your child, a good example; to a father, deference; to your mother, conduct that will make her proud of you; to yourself, respect; to all men, charity."

11

Letting Go

The less you carry, the farther you go. So let go!

The head of the monastery and his disciple had finished looking after the sick, so they left the village and headed home. After a 45 minute trek in the woods, they came to the most difficult part of their journey, a wide, raging stream that had to be crossed. But today was different, for standing close by was a lovely maiden that also wanted to cross so that she could visit her uncle who lived on the other side.

Sensing her distress, the head of the monastery approached the young lady and said, "If you can place your trust in me, I will carry you across the stream." She agreed and thanked him. He scooped her in his arms and entered the stream, followed by his disciple. Although the ten-minute trip across was arduous, they arrived safely. The elderly monk put her down, said farewell, and he and his disciple continued on their way to the distant monastery.

An hour and a half later, they had finally reached the gateway to the monastery. But instead of being relieved, the disciple appeared agitated. When he was asked what was wrong, the disciple replied, "Master, as monks we have taken vows to never touch women. Yet, you carried the maiden in your arms." "Yes, I did," answered the master, "but I put her down ten minutes later. It is YOU who are still carrying her."

Like the disciple, many of us refuse to put down what is troubling us. We carry resentment, anger, hostility, mistrust, suspicion, grudges, fear, anxiety, worries, and other burdens. How can we travel very far if we are weighed down by so many concerns? When will we learn to drop our cares, release our worries, and let go of whatever is troubling us?

We mistakenly believe that we are held captive by our emotions and impulses, unable to act as we choose. We are like prisoners in a cell that is unlocked. We refuse to leave because we falsely believe the cell protects us. Fear is an example. Although it limits us, holds us back, and blocks our progress, we refuse to let it go. We cling to it, believing that it protects us. Protects us from what? Well, what if we were to try to reach our goal and then fail? Rather than experience the pain of a possible failure, we seek shelter in the arms of fear. For if we are too scared to act, we will be protected from the pain of failure.

We cling to our negativity; we cling to what is holding us back, just as a child clings to a security blanket. But what we cling to is needless, useless, and destructive. Of what use is regret, other than having something to wallow in? Of what use is jealousy and envy other than a venue for self-pity? Of what use is anger, other than trying to control people or events? But happiness is not found in controlling others or events; it is found in controlling ourselves. And the best way to control ourselves is to loosen our grasp, to let go of our worries, and free ourselves from the bondage that disguises itself as protection.

What good is worry? It doesn't empty tomorrow of its sorrow, but today of its strength. The idea of letting go of our worries isn't new. It is part of perennial wisdom, part of the Wisdom of the Ages, part of the Wisdom of the Sages, and part of the Wisdom of the Mages. Put some magic in your life by practicing it. A good way to start is by heeding the advice of

Quintus Horatius Flaccus (65 ~ 8 BC), the Roman poet known as Horace, "Happy the man, and happy he alone, He, who can call today his own; He who, secure within, can say: 'Tomorrow do thy worst, for I have lived today.'" It is easy enough to talk about letting go, but how does one begin to do so? Some steps you can take appear below.

1. Before our world can change, we have to change. Before we can change, we have to do something different. And before we can do something different, we have to learn something different. What we have to learn is EVERYTHING IS AS IT WAS MEANT TO BE. So, accept it. At first, you may not like it, but by accepting it you can develop discipline, patience, and your threshold for tolerance. As you change your attitude by accepting what was meant to be, you eventually will arrive at a higher level, where you rejoice in everything that is; after all, everything is here for your own good. Start, then, by understanding these simple principles of life. But remember, knowledge has little value as information; its power lies in transformation. Use it to change.
2. Focus on whatever is troubling you. Don't try to run from it or hide from it. Allow yourself to feel it in its full intensity, for change is what happens when the pain of holding on becomes greater than the fear of letting go.
3. Ask yourself, "Can I let go of this feeling?" Realize that you are not your feelings and they are not holding on to you. It is the other way round; you are clinging on to them.
4. Now ask yourself, "Am I willing to make the decision to let it go?"
5. Then ask, "When will I let go?"
6. Practice this visualization technique. Imagine that the troublesome emotion is squirming, writhing, and twisting in

your hands. Feel it slithering in your hands and see yourself releasing it. Drop it. Let it go. Watch it fade away into the distance.

7. Repeat the above steps as often as needed.

The power of the above steps lies in the fact that by following them, we are putting ourselves in control. Usually, rather than analyzing our feelings and the consequences of following them, we merely acquiesce, allowing them to take us wherever they wish. By using the rational part of our brain, we remain in charge of our destiny.

12

Liberty and Freedom

Liberty, license, and liberation

LIBERTY is either granted to you by the government and others or usurped by the population in a revolution. It is a state of life in which one has freedom of expression, religion, and the pursuit of happiness. It is freedom from oppression and tyranny. A free society invites everyone to reach his or her potential. But to preserve equilibrium, freedom is carefully balanced with responsibility. We are free to pursue our dreams as long as they do not impinge on the legitimate rights of others. If I wish, for example, to become rich, I am free to work hard to do so, but not free to steal your money.

LICENSE is freedom without responsibility. It is doing whatever one pleases in complete disregard for the rights of others. In the minds of some, freedom means to be free from the need of regulations, rules, and responsibilities. If everyone felt this way, we would live in a world of anarchy and chaos. License destroys freedom, for in a world of license, no one can be trusted. The streets are no longer safe, and everyone becomes a prisoner of fear.

LIBERATION is the result of being emancipated or set free. It can be political. For instance, victims of prejudice and child abuse should be liberated so they can live their lives without fear. Since my column deals with personal development, not politics, my use of the word freedom refers to liberation from destructive habits, self-defeating attitudes, and limiting beliefs.

How ironic it is that though most of us are raised in free societies, we are prisoners of self-doubt and fear. We become immobilized by worry and disheartened by every difficulty we face. We become weighed down by responsibilities and find them overwhelming. How can we cope when we are drained of hope! When I speak of freedom, I speak of freedom from fear, doubt, regret, anger, hopelessness, and a sense of powerlessness. Liberation is a process of breakthrough and renewal. By conquering our fears and weaknesses, we become emancipated. We shatter our shackles and discover freedom.

How do we begin the process of liberation? We start by doing whatever is RIGHT, not whatever is EASY. What is right? Whatever helps us to GROW. By grow, I mean to grow BETTER. We are programed for endless growth. Frustrating this inner urge leads to a host of problems. As long as you make it your credo to be better each day than you were the day before, you will be progressing on the correct path.

In order to grow, a snake has to shed its skin. Similarly, as we grow we will do a lot of shedding. For as we continuously do the right thing, we will automatically shed worry, regret, fear, anxiety, shame, guilt, despair, doubt, and other self-limiting feelings and beliefs. After all, if I do what is right, what is there to regret? What is there to be ashamed of? If I always do the right thing, the consequences of my actions will always be positive, so what is there to worry about? This is what I meant when I wrote, "Be accountable for all your actions. When you can live with their consequences, you will know what it is to be free."

Does freedom mean to be free to do what one wants? Not in the sense of license, but it does mean to be free to do what one REALLY WANTS. And what is that? All we really want is to be happy. But some of us are confused and misled and search for happiness in all the wrong places. A 16-year-old girl, for example, engages in sex with the hope of finding love and happiness. Instead, she becomes a teenage single mom with huge difficulties, which she may or may not be able to overcome.

Yet, when we always do the right thing, we get what we really want, which is happiness. For happiness is not something found outside us. Rather, it is what remains after shedding our negative beliefs and feelings. Doing the right things, and the consequences that follow, destroy self-doubt and dissolve hurtful emotions. As we grow, we feel increasingly in charge of our life, increasingly in control. And as we empower ourselves, we experience more and more freedom.

Ralph was held back by his shyness. He decided to do something about it; he started with baby steps. Little things like smiling and saying, "Hi" to strangers in the elevator and at the lunch counter. Gradually, his confidence grew until he gained enough courage to do whatever he wished, which included leaving his company for a better job, meeting, dating, courting, and marrying a wonderful woman.

It may appear that Ralph experienced a gradual growth in courage. But that is not really the case. What actually happened is he experienced a growth in AWARENESS. You see, each courageous step he took did not add to his courage, but merely made him more aware of the courage already present in his spirit. When we believe we are separated from or APART FROM God, we may doubt our power, but if we realize that we are A PART OF God, then we will have an unlimited reservoir of resources to draw upon.

To maximize your freedom, here are two more points to keep in mind. First, at every moment, at this very moment, you are standing at a crossroad. One path leads to more of the same. The other path is one of renewal and change. One path points to the easy way, the other to the right way. One path is about existing, the other about living. One is the path to survival or getting by, the other is the path to growth, freedom, and joy.

The second point is to understand that whatever is possible is not dependent on what we used to be or what we are today. That is, at any moment we can break away from our past and embark on a new journey, the journey of infinite possibilities. It is only when you follow this path that you will discover TRUE freedom.

13

Life Balance

Happiness is not a matter of intensity but of balance

There are two main ways to balance life. Since life coexists with time, the first way to balance life is to balance time. To learn how to develop your time management skills, there is no finer book than *"The 10 Natural Laws of Successful Time and Life Management"* by Hyrum W. Smith (Warner Books, 1994). The second way to balance life is by balancing our attitude, perspective, or worldview. And we do that by avoiding extremes and taking the middle path. For instance, extreme political views, whether to the right or left, are divisive, but moderate or centrist views are unifying.

We move ahead in life by setting goals and we live a balanced life by setting goals for all our roles. Let's start by looking at our major roles in life and follow that by steps we can take to get a better balance. CAREER: provides us with the opportunity to earn income, express our personality, and develop our potential. FAMILY: provides us with the chance to express love, assume and share responsibility, and contribute to society. SPIRITUALITY: an opportunity to tap into a power greater than ourselves and a source of inspiration. An appreciation of morality, the arts, wonder, awe, and nature will heighten our awareness of the spiritual dimension. FRIENDS: an opportunity to practice sharing and caring, as well as baring our soul. SOLITUDE: quiet time to recharge our batteries, meditate, and make plans. Also, a time to work on improving our emotional and intellectual development. A time set aside to work on self-improvement. FINANCIAL: where we plan for the purchase of a car, home ownership, family vacations, and a retirement income. LEISURE: fun and recreation release steam and provide opportunities to socialize and develop new skills. HEALTH: an important component of mind, body, and spirit balance. Exercise, a proper diet, and sufficient sleep are the ingredients to success in this area.

Now, for some steps you can take to increase the balance in your life. 1) List your various roles and show by percentage how successful you think you are in fulfilling that role. For example, CAREER, 80%; FAMILY, 60%; HEALTH, 40%, and so on. Bringing the present state of imbalance into your awareness is the first step in changing the situation for the better. The areas with the lowest percentage are the areas that need the most work. The areas with the highest percentage show where you are devoting most of your time.

2) Decide how you can divert time from high percentage areas to low percentage areas. As an example, you may want to divert time from your CAREER to your FAMILY. You can do this by eliminating wasted time, developing your time (life) management skills, working more efficiently, and wresting control of your job rather than letting it control you.

3) Whenever possible, perform several roles at once. For example, if your family joins friends for a volleyball game at the park, you can fulfil several roles at once: LEISURE, FAMILY, FRIENDS, HEALTH (exercise), and SPIRITUALITY (by getting in touch with nature and enjoying a sunset in the park). Moreover, if your friend is from work, you would develop your CAREER role as well.

4) Take control of your life by making deliberate choices. Carefully weigh the costs of living with imbalance. Take

corrective action where necessary, and regularly monitor and fine-tune your progress.

5) Remember, we are all unique. It is unreasonable to expect everyone to perfectly balance each role in life. After all, part of our uniqueness lies in how we interpret what roles are the most important to us. Great artists, for example, may be consumed by their craft, spending little time elsewhere. Yes, their lives are imbalanced, but of great value to society. So, the important lesson is not about balancing our lives perfectly, but about balancing them in a manner that best expresses our potential and role on earth.

6) Follow the simple laws of BE, DO, and HAVE. You've got to BE self-disciplined to DO the necessary steps to balance your life. And when you do so, you will HAVE balance, peace, and contentment.

7) Here is some good advice taken from *"How to Be a Happy Parent...In Spite of Your Children,"* written by Fred G. Gosman, "Finding the perfect balance is getting harder and harder. We need to teach our children to be cautious without imparting fear, to learn right from wrong without being judgmental, to be assertive but not pushy, to stick to routines without sacrificing spontaneity, and to be determined but not stubborn."

What happens if you're on a plane with your child and oxygen masks suddenly pop in front of both of you? The answer is, put on your mask first, then your child's. After all, an unconscious parent is no help to a child. Because we cannot help others until we help ourselves, it is important to balance our lives. It is only after doing so that we can maximize our contribution to our family, friends, and society. How do you know when your life is balanced? If you can die today, contented with your life, it is balanced!

14

Life is Full of Surprises

Life is full of surprises, and you're one of them

Life is full of surprises, and you are one of them. I'll begin by offering two reasons YOU are so surprising. The first deals with your relationship with the universe. Although the size of the universe can be measured, its vastness is unfathomable. Nevertheless, I'll try to paint a picture of its size. Imagine gathering all the beaches on earth and placing them in one pile. The pile represents the universe and a single grain of sand, the sun. What about our planet, earth? To represent it, you would have to use a speck that is 1/300,000th the mass of a single grain of sand. Can you see why finding a needle in a haystack is infinitely easier than finding planet earth in the universe? But wait a minute, if our planet is 1/300,000th the mass of a grain of sand, what size would you be? The answer is: so small and insignificant that, as far as the universe is concerned, YOU DON'T EXIST! Yet, you do! That's what's so surprising.

Ready to move on to surprise number two? What are the odds of you being born? Before answering that, let me paint another picture. Pretend that somewhere in Canada, United States, Mexico, Central America, or South America there is the perfect mate for you. And pretend that every single member of the same sex as you, in all the above regions, regardless of their age, are striving to marry the same person you want as a mate! Since the total population for the above areas is about 765,873,947 and about half are the same sex as you, you would have to compete with roughly 382,936,973 people for the same mate! Imagine how incredibly lucky you would have to be to marry the person of your dreams. Getting back to the question I posed earlier, what are the odds of you being born? Well, very similar to my illustration of millions of people competing for the same mate. You see, before YOU were conceived, there were between 300 and 400 MILLION sperm (spermatozoa) competing to fertilize one egg (ovum)! Depending on which sperm fertilized the egg, a completely different person would have been created. So, the odds of YOU being born are one in three or four hundred million! Considering the odds, I find our existence quite surprising.

Now you know what I mean when I say that life is full of surprises and you are one of them. Someone who agreed with this assertion was the English biologist, Lewis Thomas (1913 - 1993), who wrote, "Statistically, the probability of any of us being here is so small that you'd think the mere fact of existing would keep us all in contented dazzlement of surprise." Apparently, George Burns' great love, Gracie Allen (1906 - 1964), also agreed, for she said, "When I was born I was so surprised that I didn't talk for a year and a half."

The world we live in consists of order and disorder. The laws of nature are evidence of order. The many laws are so dependable that we often forget about the chaos in our midst. Yet, uncertainty, unpredictability, randomness, the unanticipated, and the unexpected are equally enmeshed in our lives. Unfortunately, the words we use to describe chaos evoke negative images such as insecurity and instability. However, if we refer to chaos as SURPRISE, we are more likely to discover its beauty. After all, we love surprises, such as the surprise endings of stories and jokes. Why, at my last birthday, close friends surprised me by the absence of a party. Wow, what a surprise that was!

A hike in the woods is the perfect place to experience life's dance of order and disorder. Maple leaves turn crimson and fall from trees as ordained by the laws of nature. But what shade of crimson? And in which direction will they fall? Like the forest, our life will have its share of order and chaos. Chaos is to order what energy is to matter, they are just different expressions of a single principle. When we understand life, we expect the unexpected.

You're resting under a tree when suddenly, plop, a caterpillar drops on your hand. What do you do? Brush it aside? A child would never do so. Instead he or she would take a close look, trying to decipher the wonder and mystery of life. We need to regain that spirit of adventure. When disaster strikes, why do we moan about our pain instead of grabbing hold of life. As Ralph Waldo Emerson wrote, "When a resolute young fellow steps up to the great bully, the world, and takes him boldly by the beard, he is often surprised to find it comes off in his hand, and that it was only tied on to scare away the timid adventurers."

No, it is not misfortune, insecurity, and the unexpected that need to be confronted, but SURPRISE that needs to be embraced, for it is a doorway that leads to a better you. Here's how Robert D. Ballard expressed the same idea, "Everyone is an explorer. How could you possibly live your life looking at a door and not open it?"

SURPRISE is life tickling us. It is a source of joy and delight. A life without surprise, is a life of boredom. We don't have to wait for surprise to appear. We can add excitement and pleasure to life by creating our own surprises. Opportunities abound. Interested in another position, but afraid that if you applied you would be turned down? Apply anyway. For if you do, you will experience surprise. What kind of surprise? They may hire you!

Wow, that would be a nice surprise. If they don't, you will be surprised by the courage you displayed and delighted by your newfound strength. Look for areas in which you can improve and surprise yourself by creating a better you.

Share the pleasure of surprise with others. Surprise your spouse, family members and friends. Surprise your boss by showing up on time! What exotic dishes haven't you tried? Surprise yourself and friends by trying new types of food. Mmmm, delicious! Do you have some favorite hangouts? A pub, bar, coffee shop, or restaurant? Why not explore a new neighborhood? Surprise yourself with a different mood, crowd, and atmosphere. What about your tastes in music and the arts? Isn't it true that if you tried something different you may be delightfully surprised? The same is true with books, as we venture into new fields, surprising new worlds open. So, let's welcome the uncertainty of life by using surprise to uncover new opportunities, recover the wonder of our youth, and discover the joy of life.

15

Life is Unfair

Life is unfair. And it's not fair that life is unfair. (Edward Abbey, 1927 ~ 1989)

Yes, there are injustices. Guiltless people are sent to prison. Terrorists make plans to strike at innocent citizens. Facts regarding the poisons in our food are hidden from us. Olympic medals and Academy Awards are presented for political reasons instead of merit. To rise up and fight against these and other forms of inequity is not only proper, but ennobling. We should welcome the chance to make the world a better place for our compatriots and for those who follow us.

In the examples given above UNFAIRNESS is synonymous with INJUSTICE. In the case of injustice, there is always evidence supporting the claim of wrongdoing. However, very often those who complain that the world is unfair are really speaking about personal feelings, not about injustice. That's because three-quarters of what we see is behind our eyes. That is, it is in our mind. Instead of experiencing the world, we experience what we IMAGINE the world to be. For example, Tom's boss promotes another person in his department. Why didn't the boss promote Tom instead of the other person? "It's so unfair!" complains Tom.

His complaint makes it sound like he's interested in justice, doesn't it? But how can someone who seeks undeserved benefits, rewards, or recognition be interested in justice? Samuel Butler (1835-1902) described how Tom, and others like him, interpret fairness, "Justice is my being allowed to do whatever I like. Injustice is whatever prevents my doing so." All too often those bemoaning the unfairness of the world are just whining that they're not getting their way. They haven't grown up yet. Their sense of unfairness is irrational because it is based on childish demands and unrealistic expectations. They want to return to the time that they were infants. For then all they had to do was cry (complain) and someone would come and attend to their needs.

If we catch ourselves harboring unjustified thoughts that the world is unfair, it's time to change our views. Why? Because such views are unproductive. They are self-defeating. Complaining about not having what I want prevents me from getting what I want. Second, such a dark view of life is unharmonious and disrupts relationships. After all, if I resent and envy the success of others, I will be unable to maintain a warm relationship with them, separating myself even further from success.

So, how do I avoid being sucked into a downward spiral of frustration, envy, and grief? How do I escape the dead-end street of childish demands? Some suggestions follow.

1. Wake up. Whack yourself on the side of your head. Tell yourself, "Hello! The world doesn't owe me a living. If I am unhappy with my present situation, I have to accept responsibility and start creating the life I wish to live." Instead of looking for someone to blame for your unhappiness, look for solutions. Ask yourself, "What am I doing wrong? What are my options? How can I make myself worthy of what I seek?" Complaining is a dead-end street. Make a U-turn and find your way out by looking for solutions, making a plan, and taking action.
2. Work with, not against others. If you have goals and wishes in the workplace, communicate, negotiate, and ask what is necessary to get what you want. Talk about what you want,

not about what is 'fair.' Don't forget that 'fairness' is subjective, so try to see the other person's viewpoint. Remember, too, that those you work with also have goals, wishes, and rights. So, be willing to cooperate and compromise. Don't demand what you want, earn it. Instead of win-lose situations, always look for win-win opportunities. Help others get what they want. That's accepting responsibility for being a team member. When you help others to succeed, they will do likewise for you.

3. Think with your head not your feelings. Those who succeed, think things through. We make plans and formulate strategies with our brain, not our feelings. If any negative feelings arise, challenge them. Just because the boss scowled at me, I don't have to jump to the conclusion that he is angry with me. Any number of things can cause him to frown. Negative feelings and the thoughts associated with them can cause me to arrive at false conclusions and experience unnecessary apprehension. While negative emotions such as fear and anger will halt our progress, positive emotions, such as compassion, will pave the way toward success. For example, if a compassionate person sees his boss scowl, without thinking, he will immediately say, "What's wrong, boss? Is there something I can do to help?" Won't his compassion transform a negative situation into a positive experience?

4. Count your blessings, not your grievances. How can I take advantage of the opportunities that surround me if I am unaware of them or blind to their presence? Moaners and complainers see nothing but lack. Lack of opportunities, lack of 'fairness,' and lack of cooperation. They have never outgrown their childhood concept of 'fairness.' They still remember when mommy divided the cookies evenly among the children. Everyone got the same amount. Now that's fair! Like children,

they expect their boss to distribute the payroll evenly, without regard to merit. Once they start counting their blessings instead of their complaints, they'll begin to make progress.

5. Choose preferences, not demands. Those who remain immature and go through life demanding that the world cater to their every wish, set themselves up for disappointment, frustration, and resentment. Only those who are balanced and realize that things will not always go as they would like can experience peace and happiness. They realize that storms will break, fires will rage, and tragedies will descend. They prefer to avoid disaster if possible. However, if it's unavoidable they will accept it and, like countless others before them, overcome it and grow stronger because of it.

Finally, here's some additional worthwhile advice taken from the 2001 Message of the Dalai Lama (Tenzin Gyatso).

When you lose, don't lose the lesson.

Don't let a little dispute injure a great friendship.

Judge your success by what you had to give up in order to get it.

When you realize you've made a mistake, take immediate steps to correct it.

Take into account that great love and great achievements involve great risk.

Remember that not getting what you want is sometimes a wonderful stroke of luck.

Follow the three R's: Respect for self, Respect for others, Responsibility for all your actions.

Live a good, honorable life. Then when you get older and think back, you'll be able to enjoy it a second time.

16

Life Planning

Your life can't go according to plan if you have no plan

Happy New Year! Before you start making resolutions, why not make a plan? After all, your life can't go according to plan if you have no plan. Without goals and plans to reach them, you are like a traveler lost in the wilderness without a map. It's time to map out your future, for success comes to those who plan. What happens to those who don't? Well, Ben Franklin (1706 ~ 1790) has the answer, "By failing to prepare, you are preparing to fail."

A poor plan, however, can do more harm than good, so don't act too quickly.

For as Matthew Prior (1664 ~ 1721) wrote, "Who walks the fastest, but walks astray, is only furthest from his way." Therefore, take your time and be thorough. On the other hand, don't get stuck in the planning stage. Don't become paralyzed because your plan isn't perfect. Just make sure you have a clear destination in mind and have listed all the steps you have to take to get you where you want to go. To help you get started on your way, here are some goal setting tips.

1. Write down your goals. Doing so helps you to focus on them. As you write them down and refer to them in the future, they will clarify in your mind and lead to new insights. Always ask yourself what you want from life, what

is preventing you from getting it, and what are you going to do about it. Use the power of questions to develop your plan.

2. Define your goals. Get down to specifics. Be precise. Avoid vagueness. For example, "I want to be rich" is a poor goal because your subconscious does not know how to define "rich." Your subconscious can be a powerful ally in helping you achieve your goals, but it needs to be told precisely what you want. "I want to earn more money" is another example of a poor goal. Why? Because merely earning one dollar a month more than previously would result in successfully achieving your goal! So once you did so, your subconscious may stop looking for more ways to earn money. Here is an example of a good goal, "I want to earn $170,000 a year by age 40." Make all of your goals equally clear.
3. Set goals that make you stretch. If you're overweight, trying to lose one pound a year is an example of a poor goal. To be worthwhile your goals should lead to significant improvement. But don't overreach either. Trying to lose ten pounds a week, for example, would most likely lead to failure. Far better to set your goal to one pound a week. Overreaching ends in failure, while goals that are too easy prevent growth. Strive for balance. Your goal should stretch you, yet be attainable.
4. How will you benefit from achieving your goal? Why is it important? Write down the answers to these questions and keep them handy. Why? Well, there are two voices in your head, and both are saying, "I want." One is saying "I want to do what feels good" and the other is saying "I want to do what is best for me, even if I have to make an effort to do so." Both voices are competing for your attention. One is focused on immediate gratification. It is the voice that urges you to avoid your responsibilities and seek pleasure. For instance, if

it is time to go to the health club to exercise, the voice may say, "I can go next week. Instead of exercising, I want to watch TV, or go drinking with friends, or go shopping, or take a nap." To avoid listening to the wrong voice, refer to your answers to the two questions mentioned above. Focus on the benefits and remind yourself why it is important to maintain your exercise program. Focusing on the reasons to change will help you to stay motivated.

5. Set deadlines. Without a date, it's not a goal, but a wish. Each step you have to take to reach your goal should have a completion date. Each task is a mini-goal, and as one is completed, the next one begins. Each task or step you take brings you closer to your goal. As long as you keep taking steps, it is impossible not to reach your destination.
6. Subject each goal to a reality check. Are you fully committed? Are you willing to do whatever it takes to succeed? Do you understand that anything worthwhile needs some effort to achieve? Are you willing to pay the price? If not, instead of wasting time, switch to a goal that you can commit to.
7. Make sure your goal is measurable. That is, you need to have a way of measuring success. For instance, your goal may be to lose 1 ~ 2 pounds a week, drink 8 glasses of water a day, walk 10 miles a day, or read 10 pages of a book each day.
8. What are the obstacles you have to overcome? How will you overcome these roadblocks? What other hurdles could appear and how will you get over them?

   Anticipating and preparing for the obstacles you are likely to face will increase your likelihood of success.
9. Plan your work; then work your plan. If your plan is completed, carry it out. Put it into action. Implement it. No

matter how small, do something each day to bring you closer to achieving your goal. Check off each task as you complete it. Seeing your own progress will inspire you to continue.

10. Regularly monitor your progress. Life is synonymous with change. Expect the unexpected. Changing circumstances may make it impossible to stick to your original plan. Remain flexible. Look for options, solutions, and opportunities. If you can't do the best thing, do the next best thing. Adjust and adapt your plan when necessary. You can change your direction as often as you wish, as long as you keep moving forward (closer to what you want or what is possible). Review your goals daily to remain focused on them.
11. Persist. If you persist, it is impossible to fail. In fact, failure doesn't exist, only learning experiences exist. If you learn from your mistakes, they become stepping-stones to success.
12. Nothing succeeds like success. Let your achievements fan the flames, keep you motivated, and spur you on to bigger and greater goals.

It may seem like many steps to take, but the prize is most certainly worth the effort. Also, the job of planning your life can be made much easier with the help of some software.

Finally, I'd like to leave you with these words of inspiration, "Plan more than you can do, then do it. Bite off more than you can chew, then chew it. Hitch your wagon to a star, keep your seat, and there you are." Just do it!

17

Life's Little Pleasures

He enjoys much who is thankful for life's little pleasures

We call it by many names: happiness, gladness, delightfulness, or cheerfulness. I simply call it joy. What is it? It is the act of rejoicing in life's little pleasures. It is not a feeling, but a celebration.

Today, the third day of spring, it was so bitterly cold that the snow was reduced to a fine powder. As I brushed it off my car, I watched it swirl around in the wind, glisten in the morning sun, and, like winter, slowly fade away. The grains or flakes of snow may be small, but they can quickly pile up and cover the landscape. So it is with life's little pleasures. They may be little, but they are not without significance. They pile up, swirl around us, and bathe us with joy. Anais Nin (1914-1977) describes this experience: "A leaf fluttered in through the window this morning, as if supported by the rays of the sun, a bird settled on the fire escape, joy in the taste of coffee, joy accompanied me as I walked…"

Imagine a deaf and blind man seated in a movie theater. Unaware of the drama unfolding on the screen, he sits bored. Like that man, we also are sitting in a theater. And the movie that is playing is called MY LIFE. If we're unaware of what's going on, why be surprised that we're bored? But if we open our hearts, minds, and senses to life as it whirls around us, how can we be bored? Its many twists, turns, and surprises are more than enough to keep us in suspense and fill us with delight. Don't fall asleep or you'll miss all the excitement!

Take the time to enjoy the little things, such as watching the crimson sun melt into the sea, catching a baby's first smile, observing a squirrel climb down a tree headfirst, listening to birds warble against a backdrop of splattering rain, and falling asleep with your limbs still intertwined with those of your spouse. We need to do or experience something everyday that makes our souls sing. When we do so, others will enjoy our song.

Experiencing the little pleasures is merely about being attuned to life. I like Robert Holden's description of someone who is: "First you believe, and then you see the Light. Next, you go toward the Light. Soon, you are in the Light. Now you are the Light." Any suffering that comes our way never discourages a joyful soul. After all, to enjoy the better things in life, don't we first have to experience the things they are better than? Not to be joyous is almost to be sacrilegious, for as The Talmud teaches, "A person will be called to account on Judgment Day for every permissible thing he might have enjoyed but did not."

Life is not permanent and neither is any particular joyous experience. That knowledge allows us to relish it. But if we vainly try to cling to it, we will be let down. Not only will the joyous event end, but our disappointment will extinguish any hope of recognizing the next little pleasure. So, never try to hold on to the joys that come your way, but always remain open to receive their replacements. As long as you let go of any wish to hold on to life's little pleasures, you will overflow with an endless stream of joy.

Here are the comments of two poets on the same subject. "All human joys are swift of wing, For heaven doth so allot it; That when you get an easy thing, You find you haven't got it." (Eugene Field, 1850 ~ 1895). "He who binds to himself a joy doth the winged life destroy. But he who kisses the joy as it flies, lives in Eternity's sunrise." (William Blake, 1757 ~ 1827). Enlightened travelers of life don't cry because joy fades, but smile because it happened.

There are those who are joyful, those who are asleep, and those who would steal your joy if they could. Let your light shine on those who are asleep; perhaps it will awaken them. And don't become angry with those who try to steal your joy, for if you do, you will allow them to succeed. Instead, be compassionate. They are thieves and envious because they hunger for something which they lack. If you can forgive them for trying to hurt you, you will dissolve any negativity they hurl your way. They may remain resentful, but you will be free to live with joy.

"Just play. Have fun. Enjoy the game." Isn't that something you would like to say? Those are the words of Michael Jordan, who is just playing, having fun, and enjoying the game of life. How did he reach that point? Wasn't it by taking life seriously, working hard, and practicing self-discipline? Sure, he made considerable effort, and continues to do so, but aren't the rewards worth it? If we want to live life with exuberance, it's not enough to be open to it, for we also have to be willing to pay the price. We have to be willing to work hard. Oddly enough, the hard work, over time, doesn't become 'work' anymore. Rather, it becomes another source of joy.

When you enJOY the present moment, you own it and everything you have. But those who live among countless riches without joy own nothing. They are paupers. The story of the Zen master Ryôkan (1758 ~ 1831) is an example. After returning to his hut one evening, he surprised a thief who was disappointed because there was nothing to steal. "You may have traveled a long way," Ryôkan said to the thief, "I don't want you to leave empty-handed, so take my clothes as a gift." The embarrassed thief took the clothes and fled into the night. Sitting naked and gazing at the full moon through an open window, Ryôkan muttered to himself, "Poor fellow, I wish I could have given him this beautiful moon."

Living in the present moment is the secret of joy. Is that so difficult to understand? I don't think so, for Jason Lehman was only fourteen when he wrote the following poem.

It was spring, but it was summer I wanted,
The warm days, and the great outdoors.
It was summer, but it was fall I wanted,
The colorful leaves, and the cool, dry air.
It was fall, but it was winter I wanted,
The beautiful snow, and the joy of the holiday season.
It was winter, but it was spring I wanted,
The warmth and the blossoming of nature.
I was a child, but it was adulthood I wanted,
The freedom and respect.
I was 20, but it was 30 I wanted,
To be mature, and sophisticated.
I was middle-aged, but it was 20 I wanted,
The youth and the free spirit.
I was retired, but it was middle age I wanted,
The presence of mind without limitations.
My life was over, and I never got what I wanted.

18

Little Things

Little and big, what's the difference? Little!

There's very little difference between little and big because there would be no big things were it not for the little things that created them. For example, the biggest or most important part of my life is my wife, who I met because of a little advice. "If you want to meet some nice girls, you'd better go to the dance party at the nursing college this Saturday." said a friend. Following that little bit of advice led to the most significant event in my life. I'm sure you can think of many similar examples in your own life.

That's why it's not surprising that Bruce Barton (1886 ~ 1967) said, "Sometimes when I consider what tremendous consequences come from little things -- a chance word, a tap on the shoulder, or a penny dropped on a news stand -- I am tempted to think... there are no little things."

While enjoying a cup of cappuccino with my wife at a mall coffee shop, I noticed a mother and her roughly 12-year-old daughter. They were standing side-by-side at the counter, waiting for their order. While doing so, the mother suddenly turned her head and kissed her daughter on the side of her head with a loud smack. When their drinks arrived, mom and daughter picked them up and walked away. As they went on their way, the mother playfully squeezed her daughter's cheeks.

Such small things. A kiss on the side of the head and a squeeze on the cheeks. Yet, how enormous the consequences. Is it any wonder the young girl wore a bright smile and walked with confidence? Yes, a gentle kiss and squeeze are small things, but the power of love will carry that girl through a life of happiness and success.

You have the power to behave as that mother does. That is, you have the power to do great things by doing little things. But you first have to tune in to your own power, for as Kakuzo Okakura (1863 ~ 1913) wrote, "Those who cannot feel the littleness of great things in themselves are apt to overlook the greatness of little things in others."

Although little things can lead to great things, they can also lead to terrible things. Careless people, for example, may allow a LITTLE dispute to end a GREAT friendship. To prevent that from happening, remember this poem by Julia A. Fletcher Carney (1823 ~ 1908):

LITTLE THINGS

Little drops of water,
Little grains of sand,
Make the mighty ocean
And the pleasant land.
Thus the little minutes,
Humble though they be,
Make the mighty ages
Of eternity.
Thus our little errors
Make a mighty sin;
Drop by drop the evil
Floods the heart within.
Little deeds of kindness,
Little words of love,
Make our earth an Eden,
Like the heaven above.

19

Make the Right Choices

Life's greatest gift

What is life's greatest gift? It is free will or choice. Choice is the ability to select one course of action from a set of alternatives to achieve a goal. What is so great about choice? It transforms us from dumb animals into artists. Each of us becomes another Michelangelo, for choice is nothing other than the chisel we use to sculpt our life. The chisel doesn't come free, however, for the price of choice is responsibility. But when we accept and carry out our responsibility, the reward is great. The reward is happiness.

Life is not static, it is a flow. Every choice we make leads us closer to or further from our goals. We constantly need to monitor where we are on our journey. We need to ask questions: Am I moving closer to my goals? If not, what corrective measures can I take? What action will I take now to realign myself with my goals? Choice is power. Choice is at the heart of life; it is the creative power of life.

You make choices every day, and your life becomes more convenient or comfortable because of them. For example, you decide which stores to shop at and which gas station to patronize. But the decisions we make that sculpt our lives are far more important than deciding where to shop. The more we appreciate the difference between minor and major decisions, the greater the likelihood that we will experience happiness and fulfillment.

All chess lovers realize that it isn't necessary to win to enjoy the game. The pleasure is in the playing. Life is like a chess game. Make the best moves (choices) you can under the circumstances. If you live by this rule, you will always enjoy the game of life, regardless of its outcome.

How to make the right choices

Each day, we make countless choices. How can we be sure we are making the right decisions? Here are a few suggestions:

1. Be aware of where the road leads

Choose intelligence. Not every decision we make is a moral choice. Sometimes it's just a matter of choosing between stupidity and intelligence. For example, if you are a young nonsmoker and your friend offers you a cigarette, don't take it. That would be stupid. If you're looking for the path to happiness, it is easy to find. Just avoid the paths with signs that say STUPID and follow those that say SMART. Easy enough to do, but you have to remember to check the signs before you start down a path. As Harry Emerson Fosdick wrote, "He who chooses the beginning of a road chooses the place it leads to. It is the means that determine the end."

Whenever we are at a fork in the road, we will find that one of the paths is easy to take, but that may be the only thing good about it. So, look carefully. You may find that one path tempts you and the other ennobles you. Choice the one that ennobles you. Learn how to withdraw from temptation. For as it is written in the Bhagavad Gita, "Even as a tortoise draws in its limbs, the wise can draw in their senses at will."

Besides the paths of SMART and STUPID or GOOD and BAD, there is yet another road, and it leads nowhere. It is the road of non-action. It is the path of no-choice. Whenever we face choices and refuse to decide, that refusal is our decision. By refusing, we turn over control to the tides of fate, and instead of shaping our lives, we decide to drift wherever the tides and currents will take us.

2. Do what you can

Decide what you CAN do, not what you WANT to do. Our wants are insatiable. We want to do everything. But how can we become anything if we want to become everything? Choose worthwhile goals that you have time for. Set priorities and focus on the important issues. If you run out of time before getting to the minor tasks, at least you would have done the important ones.

Choose to carry out your responsibilities not because you HAVE to, but because you WANT to. Tasks that you HAVE to do create pressure and stress. Actions that you WANT to do, lead to the joy of accomplishment and freedom from inner conflict. Choose to learn how to WANT to do those tasks that you should be doing. For in the end, you will do only what you want to do. Similarly, when you can't have what you want, choose to want what you have.

3. Look for the good

Some of us may be undergoing great hardships. But no life is so difficult that it cannot be made better by improving our attitude. No matter how dire the circumstances, if you look for some good, you will find it. But how can we find anything good if we occupy our time complaining? The rule to remember is that we are certain to find what we look for. If we search for good, we will find it. If we search for something to complain about, we will surely find it. Choose to search for good. And choose to believe something good can and will happen. Choose to live with hope, rather than despair. Don't be a dope. Learn to cope. Live with hope.

4. If you can't change the circumstances, change yourself

We cannot choose what will happen TO us, but we can choose what happens IN us. That is, we can choose to have the right attitude, one in which we view challenges as opportunities instead of problems. Choose to be positive. For example, although he became confined to a wheelchair after his accident, W. Mitchell (author, TV host, and businessman) said, "Before I was paralyzed there were 10,000 things I could do; now there are 9,000. I can either dwell on the 1,000 I've lost or focus on the 9,000 I have left."

5. Be aware of your choices

When we act out of habit rather than conscious choice, the path we're traveling on is a rut, perhaps even a slippery slope. If we don't want to end up at the wrong place, we have to be awake. We have to be aware and make our choices consciously. The best way to do this is to develop the habit of always looking for opportunities. Scout Cloud Lee also writes about conscious choice: "When we acknowledge that all of life is sacred and that each act is an act of choice and therefore sacred, then life is a sacred dance lived consciously each moment. When we live at this level, we participate in the creation of a better world."

Look around you. There are great people everywhere. Champions, victors. And they're all rooting for you. They are voting for you because they want you to win. Unfortunately, you are also surrounded by losers, people who want to drag you down. They are voting against you. Half are for you. Half are against you. How will this closely contested drama turn out? It all depends on you because you will be casting the deciding vote. The ballot is the choices you make. Be careful how you choose!

20

Looking for Opportunity

Where do opportunities come from? Don't they come from other people? Doesn't that mean that if you wish to experience more opportunities you need to experience more people? If you can step out of your comfort zone and start mingling with people you're uncomfortable with, you'll be exposed to a whole new world of opportunity.

What people are you avoiding? Are they overweight or underweight? Attractive or plain? Intellectual or uneducated? Bald or hairy? Male or female? Loud or soft-spoken? Cocky or meek? Tall or short? Take off your blinders; expand your vision; open your mind and talk to them. You are uncomfortable in their presence for a good reason. It is your Opportunity Detector alerting you of a chance to make new discoveries and experience growth.

What are snobs, know-it-alls, wise-guys, jerks, losers, and dopes? They are words used by others to describe YOU when you don't behave as they want you to. You may be guilty of doing the same thing. If so, stop the name-calling and recognize that you're merely uncomfortable when things don't go your way. At times, don't things have to go THEIR way? Don't they have a right to exist? If we can look at them in a new light and make ourselves willing to listen to their ideas, we will discover they no longer rub us the wrong way. In fact, they will rub us the right way, by polishing us and causing us to sparkle and shine.

Are you avoiding members of particular races, ethnic groups, religions, or political persuasions? If so, rejoice, for once again new opportunities await you. Benefiting by the many opportunities that surround us takes more than an awareness of their presence. It also takes humility. How can I learn if I think I already know everything? When in the presence of others, one of the best things we can do is ask questions. Questions allow others to share information and allow us to absorb it by listening.

We also find opportunities by looking for them. If we would look for them as diligently as birds look for worms, we would easily uncover them. For example, the behaviour of our children may cause us to grit our teeth. But, after reflection, we may realize they give us the opportunity to become the parents we always wish we had.

It is also helpful to examine our way of thinking. For instance, some complain there is no future in their job. Of course not, there is no future in any job. For the future doesn't lie in our job, but in us. So, if we're unhappy with where we are, we need to ask ourselves what we are doing wrong. If we do so, we'll come up with answers. We'll think of things to avoid and actions to take. Opportunities will present themselves to us. So, it's not the world that needs changing, but we.

It's not only our way of thinking, but the words we use that we should be aware of. For example, every time we say, "I don't want to" or "I'm scared to" or "I don't know how to," we are expressing discomfort or fear. In other words, those expressions are pointing to opportunities waiting to be tapped.

Johnny Carson said, "Talent alone won't make you a success. Neither will being in the right place at the right time, unless you are ready. The most important question is: 'Are your ready?'" How about you? Are you ready to associate with those you have been avoiding? Are you ready to stop talking and start listening?

Are you ready to do what you have been putting off? Are you ready to make the call, instead of waiting for your phone to ring? Are you ready to seize every opportunity, no matter how small, or how difficult? Are you willing to admit that winners are people who do the things losers are uncomfortable doing? Are you ready to discover that you CAN do what you are afraid of? Are you ready to choose between realizing your dreams and realizing your fears? Are you ready to heed your Opportunity Detector?

Marianne Williamson has this perspective to add: "Our deepest fear is not that we are inadequate. Our deepest fear is that we are powerful beyond measure. It is our light, not our darkness, that most frightens us. We ask ourselves, who am I to be brilliant, gorgeous, talented, fabulous? Actually, who are you NOT to be? You are a child of God. Your playing small does not serve the world. There is nothing enlightened about shrinking so that other people won't feel insecure around you. We were born to make manifest the glory of God that is within us. It is not just in some of us, it is in everyone. And as we let our own light shine, we unconsciously give other people permission to do the same. As we are liberated from our own fear, our presence automatically liberates others."

Finally, here is a worthwhile "Knock-Knock" story told by Norman Dale:

Knock, Knock!

"Who's there?"

"Opportunity!"

"Don't be silly — opportunity doesn't knock twice!"

21

Losing Faith

An absence of faith is like a bird without wings

"It can't be done. It's physically impossible. One would fall unconscious before it could be done." These were some of the comments of renowned athletes, coaches, psychologists, and physicians, who were discussing the possibility of running a mile under four minutes. They believed it was impossible. And as long as they held that belief, it was. Then along came Roger Bannister, a British medical student who lived by faith instead of belief. What's the difference? Belief is what others tell you; faith is what your inner voice tells you.

Unencumbered by negative beliefs and brimming with faith in himself, Roger Bannister shocked the sports world on May 6, 1954 by running the mile in 3:59.4. Suddenly, "the impossible" proved possible, and the shattering of the old belief was heard around the world. Bannister's feat was all the more amazing when you consider the following facts. 1) As a busy medical student, the only time he had to practice was during his lunch hour. He practiced every day for 45 minutes and spent 15 minutes for lunch. 2) Although the track where he broke the record was supposed to be level, it had a slight upward slope, making the race even more grueling. 3) The race took place on a windy day.

Bannister's victory destroyed the artificial barrier that prevented others from running the mile under four minutes.

After everyone realized it was now possible, it only took 46 days before the record was broken again by Australian athlete John Landy. Today, of course, "the impossible" has become a common occurrence. In fact, New Zealander, John Walker, has already smashed the four minute barrier 100 times! And Morocco's Hicham El Guerrouj has shaved the time to 3:43:13!

"He must be mad! Imagine! Mr. Edison is trying to create light in his laboratory despite two fundamental laws of physics which make it impossible. First, there can be no light without combustion. Second, there can be no combustion in a vacuum." The experts at the time may have known about physics, but they didn't understand the human spirit. The incandescent lamp was already burning brightly in the mind and heart of Edison. Because of his faith, he persisted. Until, one day, his faith unlocked the secret and achieved "the impossible."

The message is clear. Faith is like a key that unlocks our potential. It knows no doubt; hears no discouragement, and sees no insurmountable barriers. It is resolute. With faith everything is possible. That's why Christ said, "According to your faith; be it done unto you." (Matthew 9:29) Why aren't there more Roger Bannisters in the world? Is it due to a lack of faith? No, says Eric Butterworth, "There is no such thing as a lack of faith. We all have plenty of faith, it's just that we have faith in the wrong things. We have faith in what can't be done rather than what can be done. We have faith in lack rather than abundance but there is no lack of faith. Faith is a law."

Faith is the realization that we can accomplish whatever we set out to do, as long as we work at it. For as Joe Namath said, "First, I prepare. Then I have faith." People of faith realize the universe is here to support us, so they surrender to their dreams and leap into the unfamiliar without fear. American Physicist, Edward Teller explains, "When you get to the end of all the light you know and it's time to step into the darkness of the unknown, faith is knowing that one of two things shall happen: either you will be given something solid to stand on, or you will be taught how to fly."

When Henry Ford was asked if he ever worried, he answered, "No, I believe God is managing affairs and that He doesn't need any advice from me. With God in charge, I believe everything will work out for the best in the end. So what is there to worry about?" Faith in life, such as Mr. Ford's, helps us to eliminate anxiety and reach our potential. No wonder someone wrote, "He who loses money, loses much. He who loses a friend loses more. But he who loses faith loses all."

Every great endeavor flows from faith. It is only after we place our trust in our dream that we can begin to materialize it. Faith is not fanciful; it is logical, for it is based on understanding the laws of life. Ralph Waldo Emerson clarifies, "All that I have seen teaches me to trust the Creator for all I have not seen." Elton Trueblood also makes a good point, "Faith is not belief without proof, but trust without reservation." Perhaps our faith cannot move mountains. But what's to stop us from climbing them? Let's cling to our faith, for it is the dawn of a new tomorrow.

22

Lost Friendships

What color is an apple?

What color is an apple? If you said red, yellow, or green, you were thinking of just the surface of the apple and ignored most of it, which is white. Although there are big differences between apples and people, we often think about both in the same way. That is, we too often see only the surface of others. Our view of them is shallow and one-dimensional. No wonder we are not impressed by most of the people we meet. Yet, if we plunge into the depths of those we encounter, we will discover hidden treasures.

Real or fictional people are not only valuable, but are necessary, for their words and deeds instruct us. They reflect our own weaknesses and faults, as well as our own strength and potential. For example, let's see what we can learn from the characters in this ancient Hindu story.

Lord Krishna ordered a wicked king to search the world for one good person and bring that person before him. After a long search, the wicked king returned and said, "I have looked far and wide. Yet, everyone I met was deceitful, untrustworthy, and selfish. There is not a single good person that I can bring before you."

Lord Krishna then asked a kind and gentle king to search the world for one wicked person and to bring that person before him. After a long absence, the kind king returned and said, "Lord, I have failed you. Although I could find many that were misguided, misled, or misinformed, none were truly evil. When they act ruthlessly, it is out of ignorance; they are all good at heart."

See how easy it is to learn from others? I'm sure you weren't surprised the evil king couldn't find a good person and the kind king couldn't find a wicked person. After all, when we explore the world, we see what we ARE. We see what we BELIEVE. And we find what we EXPECT to find. Pierre Mac Orlan (1882 ~ 1970) understood we find what we look for because he wrote, "When you have a taste for exceptional people, you always end up meeting them everywhere."

The evil king was blinded by his own prejudices and saw only the surface of others. The good king's mind was unclouded by preconceptions, so he was able to dive into the hearts of everyone he met and discover their true nature. Yes, there is a great deal we can learn from others. However, learning isn't enough. We must apply what we learn if we wish to benefit from it.

People are treasures. But as long as they are strangers, they are undiscovered treasures. It is only after making friends that we have the chance to open the lid of the treasure chest and discover the glittering gems it contains. Anais Nin (1903 ~ 1977) writes about the value of friendship: "Each friend represents a world in us, a world possibly not born until they arrive, and it is only by this meeting that a new world is born." Although friendship may not be necessary for survival, survival is meaningless without it.

The more friends we have the richer our lives. But, the number of friends we make is limited because of many impediments that block our way. The first roadblock was already mentioned. It is our prejudices, which obscure our vision. So, we need to become aware of our narrow-mindedness and destroy it. Here's how Victor Hugo (1802 ~ 1885) makes the same point, "Superstition, bigotry and prejudice, ghosts though they are, cling tenaciously to life; they are shades (shadows) armed with tooth and claw. They must be grappled with unceasingly, for it is a fateful part of human destiny that it is condemned to wage perpetual war against ghosts. A shade is not easily taken by the throat and destroyed." Yes, destroying our prejudices isn't easy, but it is a worthwhile and necessary struggle.

Another impediment to friendship is our differences. After all, birds of a kind flock together and those that are different are usually unwelcome. Our differences are like the pits in an apple, minor irritants at first, but they are the seeds of a lasting relationship. For though it is our similarities that unite us, it is our differences that we learn from.

Yet another impediment is self-centeredness or conceit. If we are engrossed in our own imagined magnificence, how can we see the splendor of others? A pompous attitude is hardly a recipe for friendship, for as Francois De La Rochefoucauld (1613 ~ 1680) wrote, "A person well satisfied with themselves is seldom satisfied with others, and others, rarely are with them."

Friendships that are won can easily be lost because of misunderstandings and disputes. Being angry with a friend is like burning down your own house to kill a rat. Rebuild damaged relationships with forgiveness and realistic expectations. After all, people are imperfect; and that includes us. If we are to be accepted with all our faults, don't we owe others the same courtesy?

In this regard, the Greek philosopher Epictetus (55 ~ 135 AD) offers some good advice, "Everything has two handles; the one soft and manageable, the other such as will not endure to be touched. If then your brother do you an injury, do not take it by the hot hard handle, by representing to yourself all the aggravating circumstances of the fact; but look rather on the soft side, and extenuate it as much as is possible, by considering the nearness of the relation, and the long friendship and familiarity between you - obligations to kindness which a single provocation ought not to dissolve. And thus you will take the accident by the manageable handle."

If we are easily hurt by the insensitive remarks of our friends, imagine how they feel when we do the same. The truth is, we make more enemies by what we say than friends by what we do. We can win a few friends with our mouths, more with our ears, and the most with our hearts. As long as we communicate in a thoughtful and caring way, we will maintain our friendships.

Friendship is to people what sunshine is to flowers. People need nurturing. They need our friendship, so don't wait for them to be friendly, but show them how. Just as one seed will yield countless apples, one friendship will sprout countless joys. Sir John Bowring (1792 ~ 1872) instructs us how to become good gardeners, "There is in every human heart/Some not completely barren part,/Where seeds of truth and love might grow,/And flowers of generous virtue flow;/To plant, to watch, to water there,/This be our duty, be our care."

One of the mistakes we make is to forget that everyone we see will die. Because of this lapse of memory, many words and feeling that should be expressed are left unsaid. Don't save your thoughts for your friend's eulogy, but express them today. And like Benjamin Disraeli (1804 ~ 1881), let's remember that, "The greatest good you can do for another is not just share your riches, but to reveal to him, his own."

23

Loving Relationships

A life without love is a jeweled cup without wine

Everyone wants to be loved. Our desire is understandable, for love gives meaning to life and lightens our burdens. The path of love is circular and begins with our parents or caretakers:

1. They love us, thereby teaching us that we are worthy of love. 2. The feeling of worthiness enables us to love ourselves. 3. Because we have loving parents, we learn that others are worthy of being loved. 4. We then learn to love others, and they in turn love us. 5. Their love of us reinforces our sense of worthiness.

Some of us were raised in dysfunctional families and were denied experiencing the circle of love. Those who feel unloved, cease to love themselves. However, as adults we can heal ourselves if necessary. We begin by acknowledging all human beings are worthy of love. Next, we look within, recognizing our good points and our value to society. Finally, we learn to love ourselves. Once we do so, we are ready to love others and the circle of love can begin.

The three pillars of romantic love

The high divorce rate is a signal that many do not understand the nature of love, which rests on the three pillars of attitude, knowledge and understanding.

What is the right ATTITUDE? It's the awareness that marriage is meant to last until death. Therefore, the choice of a partner is taken seriously. And when problems arise, they are worked out together. An example of the wrong attitude toward love and marriage is when someone asks their "sweetheart" to sign a prenuptial agreement. Or when a couple lives together in a "trial marriage." In either case at least one of the partners lacks confidence in the relationship. Marriage is not an experiment, but a serious commitment. If you need surgery, would you pick a surgeon that was willing to conduct a "trial operation" or would you want one that was absolutely committed to your complete recovery?

Do you love the country of Bhutan? Not if you've never been there and know nothing about it. You can love only a country, or person, that you know. That's what I mean by saying love is based on KNOWLEDGE. How can one claim to be in love with someone they've just met? It is only over time (generally, at least a year) that we can get to know someone. It is also important to become acquainted with as many people as possible so we have a basis for comparison when choosing a mate. If someone tells you that they fell in love at first sight, tell them "Nothing beats love at first sight except love with insight." When someone is involved in a destructive relationship, we may say that "love is blind." However, love is never blind. It is enlightened and based on insight and knowledge. It is infatuation, lust, and "puppy love" that are blind. If a relationship is built on the sand of infatuation, why are we surprised when it falls apart?

UNDERSTANDING is the third pillar that supports love. It starts with an understanding that we are all the same. We share the same hopes and fears. Or, as Alexander Smith wrote, "Love is but the discovery of ourselves in others, and the delight in the recognition." We also understand that people cannot be changed and they are imperfect. This understanding allows us to accept the "shortcomings" of our mate. In return, our partner accepts our weaknesses. It is not a matter of forgiving each other, but of understanding each other. Benjamin Franklin also believed in the importance of knowledge and understanding, for he wrote, "Keep your eyes wide open before marriage, and half-shut afterwards."

When you are loved, you will be treated with kindness, respect, admiration, and devotion. It is impossible to express love with a clenched fist. Abuse and love cannot coexist. If someone is in an abusive relationship they should seek counseling and learn whether the relationship can be rescued. If it is to succeed, your relationship must be built on mutual admiration.

Some young people say, "I want to meet an attractive person, someone with their own transportation, and a good job." They don't yet realize that love is not about WANTING, but GIVING. Love is the gift of yourself to another. "Immature love says," according to Erich Fromm, "'I love you because I need you.' Mature love says, 'I need you because I love you.'"

Partners in a loving relationship trust each other, so they live free from fear. Also, they understand the most important thing parents can do for their children is to love each other. "Marriage is not a noun; it's a verb." says Barbara De Angelis, "It isn't something you get. It's something you do. It's the way you love your partner every day. The real act of marriage takes place in the heart, not in the ballroom or church or synagogue. It's a choice you make — not just on your wedding day, but over and over again — and that choice is reflected in the way you treat your husband or wife."

24

Making a Commitment

A good start isn't good enough

We all have flashes of insight and bright ideas. But of the countless number of inspirational moments we've had and already acted upon, how many of them have we pursued to the end? How many of them have we realized? Ideas are seeds. Locked within them is great potential. Yet, what good are seeds unless we plough, harrow, and fertilize the soil, and follow that by planting, watering, and looking after the seeds until they bloom? Great ideas often lead to good starts and bright beginnings. But good starts are not good enough, for brilliant ideas are no better than poor ones, unless we follow through.

A good idea and follow-through is an explosive combination. It is the material that is used to transform lives and change the world. The detonator of this highly charged package is COMMITMENT. It is also called DETERMINATION. Commitment means NO MATTER WHAT! And determination is a refusal to allow obstacles to stop us. Here is how this idea was expressed by the man named "Coach of the Century" by ESPN, Vince Lombardi (1913 ~ 1970), "The difference between a successful person and others is not a lack of strength, not a lack of knowledge, but rather in a lack of will." Similarly, Victor Hugo (1802 ~ 1885) wrote, "People do not lack strength; they lack will." In both cases, the word 'will' refers to commitment or determination.

Commitment is like an icebreaker going through an ice floe; it is unstoppable. The whole world steps aside when a committed person passes. Such is the power of deciding to follow through. Determination brings freedom and control. No longer buffeted by the winds of fate, committed people are guided by the power of their will. They understand that it is not faith or belief that moves mountains, but determination. "Determine that the thing can and shall be done," said Abraham Lincoln (1809 ~ 1865), "and then we shall find the way." The difference between the impossible and the possible, then, lies in commitment. Anything is possible for the determined because they reject the very notion of 'trying' and insist on doing.

Despite the jeers and skepticism of their friends, young people move to Hollywood with the dream of becoming a star. Even for those who are committed, however, not everyone will make it. You see, it is not ALWAYS true that "Where there is a will there is a way," but one thing is certain: where there is no will, there is no way. So, I admire those who set out on grand adventures and wish them well. What is the harm in trying? When shooting for the stars, they may have overreached, and 'merely' land on the moon. But isn't that a lot further than most of us venture? The problem we have is not that our aim is too high and we miss it, but that our aim is too low and we reach it. Yes, not ALL the dreams of committed individuals will come true, but rest assured neither will any of their nightmares come true.

When we commit ourselves to a cause, project, or relationship, we embark on an adventure, so how can we lose? A successful outcome is not predicated on the task as much as it is on our character. By remaining determined, we live by design, not by force of habit. Let's look at a few things that may prevent us from making a commitment and experiencing the joy we were meant to have.

1. Disappointment. A certain amount of negative feelings are inevitable, even necessary. But don't repress them or get bogged down in them. Instead, experience them, work through them, and learn from them. For example, don't allow disappointment to halt your progress. Disappointment is just a message or feedback telling you that things are not going according to plan. So, instead of quitting, find out what went wrong and what changes need to be made.
2. Lack of confidence or low self-esteem. Your experiences in early childhood may have caused you to lose confidence in yourself. If so, that is a FACT, not an EXCUSE. It's time to let go of the past, acknowledge you are an adult, and accept responsibility for your own actions. Stop chasing self-esteem because it is not a goal, but a result. It is something you win each time you reach a goal. So, stop refusing to act just because you may fail. Who cares if you fail? You don't have to win every battle, you just have to win the war. And you do so by remaining determined and plodding ahead, no matter what.
3. Rebellion. Stop rebelling. Stop getting in your own way. Stop fighting yourself. Many of us are stuck in the 'resistance syndrome.' That is, when we were forced as children to yield to the will of an adult, we expressed our autonomy by rebelling. Each time you tell yourself you SHOULD be doing something, you remember the commands you received as a child and automatically resist. You need to change your self-talk. Rather than saying, "I SHOULD go to night school to complete my degree," say "I WANT to go to night school to complete my degree BECAUSE I will be learning new things, making new friends, feeling great about my accomplishments, and improve my chances for future advancement." Recapping, SHOULDs create resistance while

WANTs dissolve resistance. Don't forget to give power to your WANTs by adding BECAUSE plus the reasons for your choice.

4. Here is another point for us to think about: follow the path of wisdom. Your life is too short to experience and learn everything by yourself. So, learn from the wisdom passed down to us. For example, consider the words of Marcus Tullius Cicero (c. 106 ~ 43 BC), "What one has, one ought to use: and whatever he does he should do with all his might." Are you using what you have, your talents, and using them with all your might? To bring this point home, let's add the comments of Orison Swett Marden (1850 ~ 1924), "The greatest trouble with most of us is that our demands upon ourselves are so feeble, the call upon the great within us so weak and intermittent that it makes no impression upon the creative energies; it lacks the force that transmutes desires into realities." If we make only half-hearted efforts, why are we surprised by half-hearted results? If we're not ready to do our best, someone else is, so we'd better be prepared to be left behind.

"Nothing great will ever be achieved without great men," said Charles De Gaulle (1890 ~ 1970), "and men are great only if they are determined to be so." How about us? Are we determined to be great men and women? Are we DETERMINED? Are we COMMITTED?

25

Making Excuses

He that is good for making excuses is seldom good for anything else (Benjamin Franklin)

Most of us are guilty of having done something we shouldn't have or of not doing something we should have. When we are questioned about our misconduct, do we accept responsibility and admit we are at fault? Usually not. Instead we make excuses. Making excuses for mistakes is not new. In fact, we can trace this undesirable habit all the way back to the Garden of Eden. For when God asked Adam if he had eaten of the tree he was commanded not to, Adam created the world's first excuse, "The woman whom thou gavest to be with me, she gave me of the tree, and I did eat." (Genesis 3:12) And when God asked Eve what she had done, she gave the world's second excuse, "The serpent beguiled me, and I did eat." (Genesis 3:13)

Excuses negate responsibility, and it is responsibility that separates man from the rest of the animal kingdom. Unlike other animals, we are responsible not for what we have, but for what we could have; not for what we are, but for what we could become. If we are to take credit for our successes, we must assume responsibility for our failures. Trying to hide our failures with excuses is like concealing a small hole in our garment with a large patch; it only makes the matter worse. This analogy is taken from Shakespeare who wrote:

"And oftentimes, excusing of a fault,
Doth make a fault the worse by the excuse;
As patches set upon a little breach,
Discredit more in hiding of the fault,
Than did the fault before it was so patch'd."

Excuses are harmful because they prevent one from succeeding. When we make excuses and repeat them often enough, they become a belief. The belief then becomes a self-fulfilling prophecy. For example, a sales rep discouraged by his poor sales starts to blame the price of his product. "No one wants to buy it because it's too expensive." he says. After repeatedly making this excuse, he begins to believe it is true. The result? Dismal sales. Compare this with a responsible sales rep. After hearing many prospects complain about the high price, he accepts responsibility. "It is my fault they are complaining," the rep says, "for I haven't justified the cost of my product by adequately pointing out its value." Once we accept responsibility, we can evaluate our actions and take corrective measures to find solutions to our problems. Excuses, on the other hand, are like stop signs; they halt our progress.

By refusing to make excuses and embracing responsibility, we reap many rewards. The successes brought by this attitude act as a foundation for self-respect, pride, and confidence. Responsibility breeds competence and power. By living up to our promises and obligations, we win the trust of others. Once we are seen as trustworthy, people will willingly work with us, for our mutual gain. So, you see, making excuses can put the brakes on our progress, while accepting responsibility can lead us to the top.

How to stop making excuses and start building a life

1. Realize that your success or failure depends on you. It depends on the choices you make. It depends on your attitude. Resolve to start accepting responsibility today. Don't find an excuse, find a way. Don't make excuses, make good. Remember what Winston Churchill said, "Responsibility is the price of greatness."
2. Beware of rationalization. We make excuses to hide behavior we are ashamed of. Rationalization is the process of trying to hide shameful conduct from ourselves. This is dangerous because we become unaware of what we are doing. However, you can fight rationalization by looking for cues. For instance, if someone challenges your conduct and you become angry, it probably suggests you are guilty as charged. Why would you get angry, if you're innocent?
3. From time to time, stop and examine your progress. Compare where you are now with where you would like to be. Ask yourself why is there a gap between these two points. Don't make excuses. Make plans and take corrective action.
4. When you make a mistake, accept responsibility; learn from it; and don't repeat it. Use your time for discovering solutions instead of inventing excuses.
5. Plant your garden of success today:

   First, plant 3 rows of peas;
   Patience
   Positive thinking
   Persistence
   Next, plant 3 rows of squash;
   Squash excuses
   Squash blame

Squash criticism
Then, plant 3 rows of lettuce;
Let us be responsible
Let us be trustworthy
Let us be ambitious
Finish, with 3 rows of turnip;
Turn up when needed
Turn up with a smile
Turn up with confidence

26

Making Good Choices

Destiny is not a matter of chance, it is a matter of choice

The American Lawyer and Politician William Jennings Bryan (1860 ~ 1925) wrote, "Destiny is not a matter of chance, it is a matter of CHOICE; it is not a thing to be waited for, it is a thing to be achieved." By "destiny" he meant our future. In other words, our future doesn't come about by chance and isn't something that happens to us.

It doesn't happen to us because we create it. We do so with the choices we make. Each choice leads to a consequence. And each consequence is one strand in the fabric of our life. Since I am the weaver of the fabric that makes up my life, I cannot blame others or events for what 'happens' to me. Some find it difficult to grasp the idea that we are responsible for what 'happens' to us.

"Look," Barbara says, "I didn't choose to be poor." "And I didn't choose to be sick," adds Christopher. "Neither did I choose to be lonely," chimes in Neil. Yes, I'm sure Barbara didn't want to be poor, but she CHOSE to spend more than she earns; she CHOSE not to set aside some money for emergencies; she also CHOSE to waste money on frivolities.

True, Christopher didn't want to be sick, but he CHOSE to eat junk food; he CHOSE to avoid exercise, and he CHOSE to spend time with friends until the wee hours of the morning instead of getting a good night's sleep. And what about Neil? No, he didn't want to be lonely, but he CHOSE to criticize others, become argumentative, and spread gossip. Is it any wonder he has no friends?

Admittedly, it may be difficult to recognize that we create what happens to us by the choices we make, but if we wish to make the most of life, we must understand this truth. Once we accept it, we become empowered. We wake up each day with the realization that what happens during the day is the result of the choices we make. It is empowering to know that at any moment we can continue doing things as we always have, resulting in more of the same, or we can choose to act differently. We can choose to be grateful instead of resentful, kind instead of nasty, and helpful instead of painful. As we change our ways for the better, our lives will improve immensely.

Another fact many find difficult to accept is that happiness, too, is a choice. Yes, no one chooses to be unhappy, but they do choose to do what makes them unhappy. For example, no one chooses to become obese, but many choose to eat too much fatty food. Since it is impossible to escape the consequences of our actions, choosing the means to an end is the same as choosing the end itself.

Happiness is a state of well-being in which we are free from fear, resentment, anger, hostility, or any form of suffering. So, if we refuse to live courageously and choose to live in fear, we are also choosing to be unhappy. Likewise, if we insist on being angry, we are also insisting on being unhappy. When we choose to suffer, we are rejecting happiness.

Does it seem strange to say we choose to suffer? Well, suffering is nonexistent in the material world. It is not part of objective reality. It is purely subjective. That is, it exists only in our mind. It is a choice we make. When I speak about suffering,

I'm not speaking about pain. Pain and suffering are different. Pain is the result of something that occurred. For example if my house is swept away by a typhoon, I will be in pain.

On the other hand, suffering is a reaction, a response to something that occurred. So, if two neighbors had their homes swept away by a storm, one of them may choose the path of self-pity: "Woe is me! Everything that I have worked hard to accumulate was lost. All my precious belongings are gone!"

Yet, his neighbor may see things differently: "How lucky I am! The lives of my wife and children have been spared!"

One of the neighbors chose to look at the bright side; the other chose to focus on the negative. One chose to be happy, the other, to be miserable. "Wait a minute! That's not fair to blame the man who is suffering," someone may be tempted to say. "After all, perhaps he is a pessimist by nature. That isn't his fault, is it?"

Well, please understand that our nature is to be what we repeatedly think, do, and believe. So, if that man repeatedly thought and acted as a pessimist would, he would then become a pessimist. However, he is the one who chose to have negative thoughts, so he is responsible for what he becomes. When pessimists react to a challenge, such as job loss, they may have an automatic negative reaction. They may act without thinking. However, their automatic reactions are based on past choices, so they remain responsible.

Besides, those who are unhappy, always have the option of asking themselves, "What am I going to do about it?" Those who choose to look for a way to solve their difficulty will find a solution. Those who refuse to ask themselves that question have also made a choice. By deciding not to act, they choose to live in denial and choose to believe they are powerless to help themselves.

If we choose to live in awareness, we will realize that no matter how great our burden may be, there is always someone else with a far heavier load to carry. Therefore, we will always have a reason to be cheerful. All we have to do is be grateful for what we have.

Yet, if you try to explain this to a friend who is whining about their personal problems, their response will probably be something like, "Oh, that's easy for you to say. You don't know what it feels like to be in my shoes." Yes, it's true, you don't know what it's like for your friend, but neither does your friend know what it is like for someone with a far greater burden. That is the problem. Your friend can FEEL his or her pain, but cannot FEEL the pain of another.

Suppose you had a magical device and said to your friend, "I am going to rotate this dial, and as I do so, your pain will increase to the level of that man who is living in circumstances 10X worse than yours. Although he lives with his pain all day, I will force you to endue his pain for only five minutes." How do you think your friend would feel five minutes later, after the pain was lowered to its previous level? Wouldn't they finally feel thankful that things are not worse than they already are?

I haven't written this story for you to share with your friend. Actually, I wrote it to share with YOU. It's just a reminder that if you ever find yourself tempted to feel sorry for yourself, look for someone with a burden far greater than yours. Carefully note what you see and take in as much detail as possible. Then, when you have a quiet moment alone, take a few deep breaths, close your eyes, and picture what it would be to live as that person. Think of everything you do during the day and imagine how much more difficult it would be for you as the other person. Place yourself in their body. Try to FEEL their pain. Finally, after doing so, open your eyes and be thankful for what you have.

CHOOSE to be aware. CHOOSE to be thankful. CHOOSE to be happy.

27

Manipulating People

When we GIVE IN to others, we GIVE UP on ourselves

I'm all in favor of kindness and service to others, but not when it means allowing others to manipulate us. Refusing to allow others to walk all over us is not about being selfish or self-centered, but of being self-aware. It's about understanding we are responsible for our own lives. If we GIVE IN to others, we GIVE UP on ourselves.

This chapter is about people manipulating others. Let's start with a definition. Manipulation is about being used, abused, intimidated, coerced, pressured, bullied, or 'brainwashed' into doing something you don't want to do. When we do something that is not in our best interest simply because we were pressured into it, we surrender our personal power and turn control over our lives to others. Unlike cats, we have only one life; so, don't turn it over to someone else.

We are here to help others, but we cannot help others until we help ourselves. How can we make others strong if we ourselves are weak? How can we teach others to defend their rights when we do not defend our own? There is enough unhappiness is the world, it needs more people spreading joy. Yet, when we do what we don't want to do, we add to the unhappiness in the world.

We help one another by engaging in a series of transactions. We make exchanges of value. For example, I agree to work for my boss and he agrees to pay me a salary. As long as he pays me, he is living up to his part of the bargain and I am obligated to work for him. But manipulation involves no exchange of value. For instance, a coworker comes up to me and says, "I'm moving into a new apartment Sunday and need a lot of help. If you don't help me move in, I'll be very disappointed." The coworker is trying to manipulate me. He wants free labor and in exchange promises not to feel "disappointed." He is acting like a child threatening to throw a temper tantrum unless it gets its way.

I'm not responsible for my coworkers' feelings. I would hope he chooses to be happy and joyful, but if he chooses to be unhappy and disappointed; well, that's up to him. Because of the absence of an exchange of any value, I am not obligated to help him. Nor do I owe him any explanation or apology. So, the conversation may go something like this:

"Sorry, Bob, but I have something else planned for Sunday."

"How long will you be busy on Sunday?"

"All day."

"What are you doing that's so important?"

"Leading my life by doing what I want to do. It's something I recommend to everyone."

"I'm disappointed in you, Chuck; I thought I could count on you."

"If you want someone to count on, call the moving company."

I'll stop here, but manipulators can be persistent. They hope you will break under the pressure. If Bob were to persist, I would just break off the conversation with something like, "Sorry, Bob, but I already gave you my answer. I wish you luck. Now I've got to get back to work. See you later." Also, when standing up for our rights, there is no need to reply in a hostile tone. We can remain polite, but firm.

Bob, my coworker, is just an acquaintance, but Jim is a friend. Compare Jim's conversation with Bob's. "Chuck, I'm getting ready to move again. I know you're working on your basement. If you give me a hand moving, I'll help you out in your basement."

There's a big difference in conversations, isn't there? That's because Jim is not a manipulator. Cooperation is the opposite of manipulation. He offered to exchange something of value. I was happy to help because we both got each other's job done in half the time and had fun doing so.

To avoid being a victim, remain on the alert. If someone asks you to do them a favor and you can't say NO without fear or YES without resentment, you are a victim. If you are, it's time to regain your power. No one stole it from you, you handed it over to them. Now take it back. After all, you can't live for others without squandering your own life. When you are in control, doing what you want to do, you will be happy and in the position to spread happiness to others. But when you reluctantly follow the wishes of others, you will be resentful and spread misery. You owe it to yourself and others to remain in control of your life.

Although you should be on the alert, there is no need to fear the attempts of others to manipulate you. For their attempts will give you the opportunity declare, decide, and develop into the person you want to be. Further, once you understand why they are trying to manipulate you, your fear will be replaced with compassion. And because of your compassion, your assertiveness will never change to aggression.

Why do some people try to manipulate others? Because they're weak. Weak people are not to be feared, but to be pitied. Their weakness comes in many forms and includes feelings of inadequacy and incompetence. They try to get others to do what they believe they cannot do. They try to compensate for their feelings of powerlessness by gaining power over others. People like this don't care which way the car is going as long as they remain in the driver's seat.

Also, people who live miserable lives like to make others miserable too. When they are successful in doing so, they find some relief by diverting their attention from their own pain to the pain of others. Also, they may be afraid that if they ask for what they want, you may refuse, so they try to manipulate you instead. Some manipulators have distorted thinking. They either believe they are superior and entitled to their demands or they feel they are treated as inferiors and therefore are entitled to special privileges.

Whatever the cause, it's based on weakness. So, whenever they try to get their way by making you feel guilty, refuse to give in to them, but do so in a gentle caring way; after all, they're weak, and you're not. When facing manipulation, don't give in to fear. Don't be afraid of losing a friend, hurting their feelings, or disappointing them. You are responsible for your life, not theirs. Remain vigilant and ignite in your heart the flame of courage, for as Helena Petrova Blavatsky (1831-91) wrote, "The more thou dost advance, the more thy feet pitfalls will meet. The Path that leadeth on is lighted by one fire — the light of daring burning in the heart. The more one dares, the more he shall obtain. The more he fears, the more that light shall pale."

28

Many Religions

To find what you search for, seek without seeking

Many people are on a quest. They are searching for answers to their QUESTions. They wonder to themselves, "Why am I here and what is the purpose of life?" Traditionally, religion has provided the answers. In ancient times, villages, towns, and even countries were isolated. One religion and culture were shared by all members of the group. The faith they held in common was all they knew. There were no reasons to question what they were taught. Today, for many, that is changed. Because of commerce, immigration, modern transportation and communication, the isolation of the past is gone. Children in remote villages can catch glimpses of faraway places on the community TV. And North Americans are studying Buddhism and practicing Tai-chi while Japanese children are being taught English by Mormon missionaries.

If you're searching for answers, do you turn to religion? If so, which one? With so many choices and different answers, no wonder people are puzzled. For example, if I wish to learn about Buddhism, should I study Nichiren, Tendai, Shingon, Zen, or Tibetan Buddhism? If I'm attracted to Christianity, should I become a Pentecostal, Fundamentalist, or Evangelical? What about Southern Baptist, United Church of Christ, Lutheran, or other Protestant denominations?

Maybe I should become a Jew. But which one: Reformed, Orthodox, or Conservative? Perhaps Hasidic? I could consider Greek Orthodox or Roman Catholicism. But how about Sikhism, Hinduism, Hare Krishna (ISKCON), The Teachings of Dadaji, Jainism, Sunni and Shiite Islam, The Bahai Faith, Taoism, Zoroastrianism, Confucianism, and Shinto.

Not enough? I can always look into the Seventh-Day Adventists, Jehovah Witnesses, Unitarians, Christian Science, Course of Miracles, The Church of Jesus Christ of Latter-Day Saints, and the Salvation Army. Or, for something a little different, I could consider Eckankar, Urantia Book Fellowship, The Unification Church, Raelian Religions, Church Universal and Triumphant, Theosophy, Adidam, Falun Gong, Children of God, Dao Cao Dai (Caodaism), La Regla Lucumi, Vodoun (Voodoo), or even Wicca and Scientology. Of course, if none of these pleased me, there are lots more to choose from!

Why so many religions? They don't descend from heaven like raindrops, but arise from the needs of man. As Emerson wrote, "Heaven always bears some proportion to earth. The god of the cannibal will be a cannibal, of the crusaders, a crusader, and of the merchants a merchant." Montesquieu expressed the same thought differently: "If triangles had a god, he would have three sides." If we seek the God who created man, instead of the god created by man, what are we to do? Can we find Him alone? I agree with Epictetus who wrote "God hath entrusted me with myself."

How do we discover God by ourselves? One way is by following the advice of the twelfth century Chinese Zen Master, Fo-Yan (1067-1120). He taught, "If you seek, how is that different from pursuing sound and form? If you don't seek, how are you different from earth, wood, or stone? You must seek without seeking." How do we seek without seeking? By stop seeking answers and start seeking experiences. God is not to be known, but to be experienced. How can a god that is small enough to be understood be great enough to be worshipped?

Man searching for God is like fish searching for water. The fish don't realize that their bodies contain water, their flesh is mainly made from water, and they live and swim in water. Are we no different from fish? Speaking on behalf of God, the Hindu Philosopher, Kabir (1400-1499), writes "Where are you searching for me, friend? Look! Here am I right within you. Not in temple, nor in mosque, not in Kaaba (the famous Mohammedan temple at Mecca) nor Kailas (the most sacred mountain in Asia) but here right within you am I."

When we are humble enough to realize that God cannot be understood, just enjoyed, the questions we had dissolve. For as Dr. Bernie S. Siegel wrote, "It is the experience of living that is important, not searching for meaning. We bring meaning by how we love the world." And when we love the world, we love the Creator of the world.

When we experience God, instead of being tortured by questions, we are enthralled by wonder. "My religion," says Albert Einstein, "consists of a humble admiration of the unlimitable superior who reveals Himself in the slight details we are able to perceive with our frail and feeble minds. That deeply emotional conviction of the presence of a superior reasoning power, which is revealed in the incomprehensible universe, forms my idea of God."

We can experience God in a grain of sand, a blade of grass, or in the sparkle of the morning dew. The poets experience God. For example, William Blake wrote, "To see a world in a grain of sand and heaven in a world flower. To hold infinity in the palm of your hand, and Eternity in an hour." And Alexander Pope penned "All are but parts of one stupendous whole, Whose body

Nature is, and God the soul." Also, Edna St. Vincent Millay wrote, "God, I can push the grass apart and lay my finger on Thy heart." Not much of a poet, but a great comic, Lenny Bruce said, "Every day people are straying away from the church and going back to God." Perhaps that's something we should think about. If you've been wondering about the answers to profound questions, you may want to redirect your focus and experience the wonder of life and the joy of mystery.

29

Meaning of Apathy

It's nothing to die; it's frightful not to live. (Victor Hugo)

What is the difference between ignorance and apathy? I don't know and I don't care. Do you realize that scientists discovered a cure for apathy? But no one cares! Lastly, a public service announcement: The Apathy Anonymous meeting was canceled due to lack of interest.

If you haven't figured it out yet, I was only joking. Yet, there's nothing funny about apathy, so let me get serious. The word has its origin in Greek and literally means "without feelings." Isn't that a description of the dead? That was what Victor Hugo was referring to when he wrote, "It's nothing to die; it's frightful not to live." In other words, we should not be afraid of dying, but not living. The apathetic are alive, but without feelings, so they are not living. They are the living dead.

Here's what the psychoanalyst Erich Fromm (1900-1980) had to say about the subject, "... In the 19th century the problem was that God is dead; in the 20th century the problem is that man is dead..." He calls apathy a problem for a good reason. It is a double-edged sword that wounds both the apathetic and the society in which they live. For example, although nuclear weapons cannot destroy democracy, voter apathy can! Such is the horrific negative power of apathy. As the world's leading democratic country, the US, prepares to go to the polls, voter turn out is expected to be about 36%. Wouldn't you call that a wakeup call?

What is the cause of apathy? It is often frustration and a sense of powerlessness that causes people to withdraw from life. However, the ultimate cause is their attitude, the way they react to the changing world. Let's take a look at a specific example.

Jan has recently learned that her company has been bought by another company. Within a month, she and her coworkers will learn who among them will be hired by the new company and who will lose their jobs. Overnight their sense of security has been shattered. They are experiencing apprehension and frustration. They feel that they have lost control over their lives. They complain and disengage from activity. "If the company doesn't care about me, why should I care about it? What's the point of working when I'm probably going to lose my job anyway?"

This is an example of worker apathy. The staff has been reduced to a bunch of zombies. No one is doing their job. They are just putting in their time until that fateful day when they learn whether they have a job in the new company. There is one exception, however. And that is Jan. She is different. She has a different attitude and is living proof that apathy is not caused by events, but by our reaction to events.

Like her coworkers, Jan was disappointed to hear the news. But she wasn't completely taken by surprise because she understands nothing is permanent, including her life. She also understands that adversity is our friend. Because it makes us stronger. their opinions. Yet, if they were to courageously give their views, they would earn the respect of their classmates and teachers. Another form of student apathy is lack of involvement in the student government and other activities. This can often be overcome by an invitation to participate by members of the faculty. When a teacher asks someone to join the student council, there is the implication that they are being asked because of their leadership qualities. This is often enough to motivate the student to join in.

The media—In their quest for higher ratings, the media keeps pushing the boundary of what is suitable for viewing. Skeleton-like starving children, people being burned alive or falling from buildings, or endless rows of bodies in a foreign battlefield. These and other images appear on our TV screens so often that they seem to represent the norm, rather than the exception. If it's normal, why be concerned? If we're not desensitized, we deliberately shut those images out of our mind to avoid the pain of thinking about the suffering of others. What the media needs to do is switch the focus from the news of people suffering to the news of people helping those who suffer. When we focus on people like Mother Teresa, other missionaries, and charitable organizations, we inspire participation rather than dropping out.

Overwhelming problems—Because of the vast number of problems facing society, we feel overwhelmed, which leads to paralysis. Peace in the middle east and elsewhere, the nuclear threat, which still remains; poverty, homelessness, crime, global warming, pollution, the growing ineffectiveness of antibiotics, corporate downsizing and reliance on part-time workers, animal rights, euthanasia, capital punishment, and countless other problems haunt us. But we need not give up. True, the limited nature of our lives makes it impossible to do EVERYTHING, but we can do SOMETHING. And if each of us were to do something, the number of problems would lessen or their effects would decrease.

We are social creatures and need one another for survival. So, let's get involved and do our part. "The world is a dangerous place to live;" said Albert Einstein, "not because of the people who are evil, but because of the people who don't do anything about it." We need to take sides and stand up for what's right. Apathy and neutrality oppresses the victims, and silence encourages their tormentors. We are guilty of complicity in the suffering of others when we are indifferent to their pain. Scientists discovered a cure for apathy. It's called involvement. Who cares? We do, so let's continue to make a difference.

30

Meaning of Perseverance

You are never a loser until you quit trying

What trait has the power to change an ordinary person into an extraordinary one? It's perseverance, also known as persistence, steadfastness, patience, or tenacity. It's the ability to hold on to your dream like a pit bull, refusing to let go, regardless of the obstacles. Perseverance is one of the secrets of success. After all, if you keep moving toward your goal, never quitting, you will eventually reach it. It's a simple, but crucial, idea. Arthur Pine expressed it well when he said, "Your biggest break can come from never quitting. Being at the right place at the right time can only happen when you keep moving toward the next opportunity." No one believed in this principle more than Sir Winston Churchill, who delivered this nine-word commencement address: "Never give up! Never give up! Never give up!"

Perseverance is necessary because anything worthwhile is difficult to do. So, we have to expect roadblocks. When you come to one, smash through it; go around it; burrow under it; jump over it; take a detour; do anything as long as you continue toward your goal. Pretend you're the Energizer Bunny and just keep going.

However, don't confuse perseverance with obstinacy. That is, don't keep banging your head against a brick wall until you smash your skull. You have to temper persistence with common sense. If you can't pass a roadblock after a reasonable number of tries, it's time to find another route. There's more than one way to reach your goal. The trouble with some people is that during trying times, they stop trying. But why should we ever stop? Isn't it true that stopping at third base adds no more to the score than striking out? Ask yourself, do we stop trying because we fail, or do we fail because we stop trying?

We have the power to persevere. It's just a matter of making up our minds to do so. It may be helpful to remember that people don't succeed because they are destined to; they succeed because they are determined to. When you come to bumps in the road and feel doubtful, say to yourself, "Cowards despair, but I persevere!"

Study the lives of others for inspiration. When the great, contemporary instrumentalist and composer, Yanni, chased his dream, he didn't let his inability to read music stop him. He still can't read, but by persevering, he put together concerts that remain unmatched in grandeur. It took two years of preparation for his 1993 live performance at the Acropolis, in Greece, which was viewed by over half a billion TV viewers, resulted in sales of seven million albums, and became the third best-selling music video of all time. The obstacles he had to overcome for his 1997 Taj Mahal and Shanghai concerts were even more daunting, but they brought this world-renowned artist even greater success.

Another musical artist that can't read music is Andrea Bocelli. But he can't read for a good reason – he's blind. Born with impaired vision, he completely lost his sight at age twelve in a soccer accident. Blind or not, Andrea went to the university and persevered, receiving a doctorate of law degree, and practiced law for a short time. However, he decided to follow his dream and become an opera singer. While singing in piano bars, he studied under Franco Corelli, a legendary tenor. Today, some call Andrea the "fourth tenor," but there is no doubt he will surpass Luciano Pavarotti in fame. Although he has sold over ten million CDs, he is still fairly unknown in North America, so he has enormous potential. He is determined to let nothing stop him from doing what he loves. Mounted on one of his Arabian stallions, he gallops along the beaches and countryside of his native Tuscany, Italy. He even goes skiing on the slopes of the Italian Alps with his Olympian friend, Alberto Tomba.

What did Yanni and Andrea Bocelli do to succeed? Persevere! And we can do the same by remembering the words of Edgar A. Guest's poem:

Don't Quit

When things go wrong, as they sometimes will,
When the road you're trudging seems all up hill,
When the funds are low and the debts are high,
And you want to smile, but you have to sigh,
When care is pressing you down a bit,
Rest, if you must--but don't you quit.
Life is queer with its twists and turns,
As every one of us sometimes learns,
And many a failure turns about
When he might have won had he stuck it out;
Don't give up, though the pace seems slow –
You might succeed with another blow.
Often the goal is nearer than
It seems to a faint and faltering man
Often the struggler has given up
When he might have captured the victor's cup.
And he learned too late, when the night slipped down,

How close he was to the golden crown.
Success is failure turned inside out—
The silver tints of the clouds of doubt—
And you never can tell how close you are,
It may be near when it seems afar;
So stick to the fight when you're hardest hit—
It's when things seem worst that you mustn't quit.

31

Meanness

The end never justifies the meanness

We recoil in horror when others commit acts of cruelty, yet we forget our own. Have you ever been tempted to give unsolicited advice to a friend? Don't do it; bite your tongue. For example, inviting a friend to join you in workouts at the health club so they can lose some weight may appear perfectly innocent, but what are you really saying? Isn't it, "You're not acceptable to me; you need some improving!" But what are friends? Aren't they supposed to be people who accept one another unconditionally? Besides, if your friend is overweight, don't you think they already know it? So, your suggestion to join you for workouts merely reminds them of their lack of self-discipline and adds to their stress. No matter how good your intentions were, the end never justifies the meanness.

Meanness? Yes, meanness. Before you dispense advice or make suggestions to a friend, ask yourself whether your comments will make your friend feel better or worse. If the answer is better, you're a friend. If the answer is worse, you're just being mean. If you want to be in the construction business, wouldn't it be better to rebuild people than to tear them down? If your friend has obvious defects, you can be sure they have low self-esteem. They need a boost in confidence, not a knife in the back. Become blind to their faults and acutely aware of their strong points. Talk about what you like about them and you'll make them feel good about themselves, as well as remind yourself of the value of their friendship.

As we go through life, we will run into much meanness. We will find it in the workplace, in the marketplace, and even in, what is supposed to be our sanctuary, own home. Why are people so nasty? Cruelty often stems from feelings of weakness, inadequateness, or worthlessness. Those who feel powerless strike out at people. They try to gain power by dominating others. Their favorite weapons are ridicule, criticism, and bullying.

Just as individuals can grow twisted and inflict great cruelty, the same is true for groups. In extreme cases they may resort to terror. For as the notorious Nazi war criminal Heinrich Himmler said, "The best political weapon is the weapon of terror. Cruelty commands respect. Men may hate us. But, we don't ask for their love; only for their fear." Although Eric Hoffer (1902 - 1983) wasn't writing about the Al Qaeda organization, his words do explain why they are so desperate to break the spirit of the United States, "Our sense of power is more vivid when we break a man's spirit than when we win his heart. For we can win a man's heart one day and lose it the next. But when we break a proud spirit, we achieve something that is final and absolute."

Terrorists justify their bloodbaths and carry them out without guilt by dehumanizing their enemy and making them objects of hate. They hate others in order not to hate themselves. When their enemies are viewed as satanic barbarians, their slaughter can even be thought of as a "holy" act. Although I am now writing about extreme acts of terrorism, they have their origin in small acts of injustice that have been allowed to fester and grow into the desperate acts of desperate people.

This is why we must be on guard, ever mindful of the hurtful acts we commit. Little acts of intolerance, for example, can spread in the community like a fire. When the victims strike back, we will then have justification for escalating the violence. And so the vicious cycle continues. Obviously, we have enough suffering in the world. Instead of fanning the flames, we need to put them out. Better yet, we need to prevent fires from igniting.

We can prevent fires from occurring by being more tolerant, understanding, and accepting. When people are cruel to us, we can forgive them for their weakness, and learn from it by examining our own behavior and vowing to ourselves not to treat others in the same fashion. Francis Beaumont (1584 – 1616), writing on the same subject, had this to say, "If men wound you with injuries, meet them with patience: hasty words rankle the wound, soft language dresses it, forgiveness cures it, and oblivion takes away the scar. It is more noble by silence to avoid an injury than by argument to overcome it."

The last sentence in Beaumont's quotation reminds me of a recent incident. At a meeting I attended, a member discussed his belief in determinism. I was dying to refute his argument by presenting powerful evidence supporting the claim that we have free will. But instead of speaking up, I bit my tongue. Why do I have to change his way of thinking, I thought. If I feel a need to change it, doesn't that imply that his thinking is inferior to mine? Isn't that judgmental? Why can't I be tolerant and accepting, I thought. So, I bit my tongue and remained silent. The person chairing the meeting, however, did speak up. She said to the speaker, "Yes, many people believe in determinism. Of course, many also believe in free will. It is GOOD that you have studied both sides of the issue and WISE that you follow the position that makes the most sense to you." Wow! What a difference in approach! While I was passive, she was active and made the speaker feel good about himself. And what she said was absolutely true; she wasn't resorting to flattery, but displaying great understanding. I learned something useful that day.

Another lesson we can learn is that when we dehumanize others, we dehumanize ourselves. Ralph Waldo Emerson (1803 - 1882) explains why, "Treat men as pawns and ninepins and you shall suffer as well as they. If you leave out their heart, you shall lose your own." On April 6, 1940, George Orwell repeated the message of Emerson. But he did so with his own dramatic story: "I thought of a rather cruel trick I once played on a wasp. He was sucking jam on my plate, and I cut him in half. He paid no attention, merely went on with his meal, while a tiny stream of jam trickled out of his severed esophagus. Only when he tried to fly away did he grasp the dreadful thing that had happened to him. It is the same with modern man. The thing that has been cut away is his soul."

Perhaps the greatest tragedy lies not in the extent of meanness that envelopes society, but in the fact that the souls who suffer do so at the hands of those responsible for their care or their friendship. Let's lessen the pain. Do you know what I mean? Don't be mean!

32

Mental Flexibility

Blessed are the flexible, for they shall not get bent out of shape

Isn't it wonderful to be mentally flexible? For when we are, we'll never get bent out of shape. But mental flexibility is much more than a desirable trait. It is essential for the welfare of humanity. Without it, we place our planet and ourselves in peril. Oppressive regimes inflict terror and deny human rights because they believe their way is the only way. Their rigidity of thought doesn't tolerate freedom of expression. Even democratic nations can get carried away. "You are either for us or against us," one says. That' s hardly flexible. It leaves no room for compromise. It does not attempt to understand the underlying causes of the problem. It is a reaction instead of a solution.

Religious institutions are no better. Claiming to be the representatives of God on earth, they act in the most ungodly fashion. Their inflexible views divide humanity into separate camps: 'true believers' and 'heathens.' Rather than embrace diversity, they seek to crush it. They have no compunction as they kill their brothers and sisters of different faiths. But why be surprised? The god they believe in is a vengeful god, a jealous god, an intolerant god.

My aim isn't to discuss religion or politics here, but to point out how critical, critical thinking is. What about our society? Do we have the ability to handle different situations in different ways? Are we able to see things from different perspectives? Can we solve problems in new ways? Can we understand and appreciate the viewpoint of others? If so, why are there so many divorces? How can husbands and wives arrive at a consensus when their thinking, attitude, and perspective are so rigid? "I'm right and you're wrong," is nothing more than an expression of intolerance, narrow-mindedness, and rejection.

Besides openness to new or different ideas, mental flexibility allows one to adjust to a changing environment. Much of the stress we experience in life is due to the inability to accept change. But accept it we must, for it is both inevitable and the very nature of life. When a Mozart symphony suddenly takes a twist in a new direction, we don't get upset because we were unprepared for it. On the contrary, we are delighted by the surprise. Life is no different. It is a symphony. Those who are flexible relish its many twists and turns, ups and downs, ambiguity and uncertainty.

There are other aspects of flexibility, such as learning from past mistakes and willingness to take risks. At times, politicians are criticized for changing their minds. "They lack consistency. They have no strength of conviction." so the argument goes. But what are minds for, if not for changing? Changing one's mind is not a sign of weakness, but of flexibility and growth. Flexibility also promotes mental and physical health because it frees us from stress, as well as toxic emotions, such as resentment, anger, and fear. To the flexible person, life is not about survival but about enjoyment.

All right, agreed. Mental flexibility is important. So what are the steps we can take to cultivate it?

1. When you're listening to the viewpoint of another and are tempted to disagree with it, remember that you will be changing your own opinion in the future. So, does it really make any sense to debate the point? Rather, remain open.

The more ideas you have to draw upon, the more flexible, creative, and solution oriented you will become.

2. Did you ever notice that the only people we consider intelligent are those that share our opinions? If so, it's time to get rid of that narrow viewpoint. When your companions give their opinions, rather than focusing on the differences between theirs and yours, focus on the differences their opinions have made in their lives. If their opinions have made them better people, it's time to think about changing your viewpoint.
3. Don't cling to your opinions, for they are nothing more than knowledge in the making, nothing more than potential truth. Remember that you don't own the truth because it is shared by all. Everyone is necessary to arrive at the big picture.
4. To benefit from the wisdom of others, don't get turned off by how they present their opinions. Focus on the substance, not on the presentation; focus on the gift, not on the package.
5. Whenever the opinions of others make you feel uncomfortable, don't run and hide. But be especially alert for hidden treasure. For whenever we are forced to step outside of our comfort zone, we grow.
6. To be flexible, we must be willing to break from tradition, custom, and habit. We must be willing to question everything. Keep an open mind, but remember gullibility enslaves you to the opinions of others, while skepticism frees you to discover the value or uselessness inherent in the ideas of others.
7. Don't rely exclusively on the left hemisphere of your brain. That is, don't depend solely on logic or rational thought. Increase your use of the right hemisphere, which is the seat

of intuition and creativity. Become more attuned to the arts, nature, beauty, and the wisdom of your inner voice.

8. Learn from any source you can. Friends, acquaintances, and coworkers. Books, magazines, and newspapers. New information is the source of new options, and new options offer greater flexibility.
9. Adjust your attitude and perspective. They filter reality, acting as colored glasses, distorting everything you see. When you begin to view strangers as friends you haven't made yet, instead of potential threats, you'll become more flexible.
10. Learn to view the world through the eyes of another. How would you see things differently if you were an infant, five years old, or a teenager? What if you were a member of the opposite sex? Or ninety years old? Or gay? What if you were confined to a wheelchair or a prison cell? What if you were raised in poverty in the third world or were homeless in North America? What if you were a faithful follower of a different religion? What if you were a traffic cop, schoolteacher, or bank teller? Use the power of your imagination to place you into as many roles as possible, for flexibility consists of understanding the viewpoints of others and learning as much as possible from them.

Would you agree that different opinions are not the enemy? Wouldn't you say that, on the contrary, they are the source of wisdom, knowledge, understanding, and power? But all that power would be denied to us unless we had an open mind. I was about to end by suggesting you rigidly adhere to the principle of flexibility, but to rigidly adhere to any principle wouldn't be flexible, would it? Anyway, you know what I mean.

33

Mental Retreat

Only eight steps away

Did you ever attend, or think of attending, a retreat? They are often run by religious groups, spiritual teachers, therapists, and others. Found in remote areas and surrounded by natural beauty, they are perfect havens, sanctuaries, and refuges from the clamor of city life. There in the midst of silence, one learns how to release stress, quiet the mind, engage in reflection, and rejuvenate the spirit.

Did you know that the nearest retreat in your area is just eight steps away?

That is, if you follow the eight steps shown below, you will be able to build your own retreat in your mind. By harnessing the power of your imagination, your mental retreat can deliver the same benefits of costly, remote sanctuaries.

The easiest way to learn the eight steps is to record them in a small, handheld, tape recorder. After, familiarizing yourself with the PAUSE (or STOP) and PLAY buttons, sit down in a quiet area where you will not be disturbed. Take a few deep breaths, relax, and press the PLAY button of the tape recorder, listening to the instructions for Step 1. Press the PAUSE or STOP button after the instructions, and carry out what you were told to do.

Repeat this for each step

Here are the eight steps:

1. CHOOSE A LOCATION. If you could choose the location for your sanctuary, where would it be? A lush deserted island? Soothing hot springs? A quiet Zen monastery? A tropical beach? A canoe floating on a placid lake? Pick a location, real or imaginary, that is comfortable for you.
2. BUILD THE PICTURE. Now that you have chosen a location, fill in the blanks with more detail. Are you inside or outdoors? Is it morning, afternoon, evening, or night? Is it spring, summer, fall, or winter If outdoors, are flowers in bloom or is a waterfall nearby? If indoors, are there chandeliers, candles, or a fireplace?
3. ENTER THE PICTURE. Place yourself in the scene. Are you sitting on a chair, on a rug, on grass, or lying in a hammock? If the sun is out, is it directly above, in front of you, behind you, or to the left or right? What are you wearing? What is immediately behind you, beside you, and in front of you? What do you see in the distance?
4. ENGAGE YOUR OTHER SENSES: a) Touch. What do you feel? Warm sand? Moist grass? Silk drapes? The warmth of the sun? A cool breeze? b) Hearing. What do you hear? Rain? Flowing water? Rustling leaves? Birds, insects, or frogs? A crackling fireplace? A creaky door? c) Smell. What do you smell? Burning wood? Incense? Grass? Flowers? Fruit? Burning candles? d) Taste. What can you taste? Cold water? Hot tea? Delicious food? Dew-soaked flower petals?
5. OVERALL SENSATIONS. Allow all the sensations of your senses to sweep over you. What are your overall

impressions? Are they delightful, delectable, pleasurable, or relaxing? Spend a few moments enjoying the pleasures of your retreat.

6. FINISHING TOUCHES. Now that you have created a wonderful retreat, how can you improve it? Should it be bigger, or would you like to make it cozier? How is the sound level? Would you like it to be quieter or would you like to boost the sound. Whether it's a piece of furniture or a waterfall, you can move things around. Keep fine-tuning your sanctuary until you are happy with it.
7. MEASURING YOUR FEELINGS. Do you remember how you felt when you first started? How have your feelings, thoughts, and sensations changed? Are you more relaxed? Have all or most of your worries and problems receded into the background? Do you have a warm tingly feeling? Did you notice your retreat grow clearer and clearer with each step? Did you experience any new insights?
8. ESTABLISHING A TRIGGER. Reexamine your sanctuary. Re-experience the sights, sounds, tastes, textures, and fragrances. Look around and pick one object that easily fits into your hand. Choose an object that you can easily identify with your personal sanctuary. This object will be used to trigger future visits to your retreat. It could be a cherry blossom, mushroom, bead, gemstone, unlit candle, or anything else that is meaningful to you. After selecting your trigger, hold it and study it carefully. Is it smooth or rough? Hard or soft? What does it smell like? Is it damp or dry, warm or cold? After absorbing the image of your trigger into your mind, return the object to its place in your sanctuary. When you wish to return to your retreat in the future, all you have to do is relax and visualize the image of your trigger. It will then propel you to your retreat. The first time you try,

you may only get partially there. That is okay, just improve the image until you are completely back. Each time you use the trigger, it will become more and more effective, so be patient.

Practical Applications

The most obvious use of your sanctuary is to have a place where you can experience deep relaxation and pleasure. It is a place where you can shed needless stress and 'recharge your batteries.' But it is more than that. The quietness of your inner sanctuary makes it easier to hear the voice of your inner wisdom. You can visit it to obtain new insights, get inspired, and obtain answers.

It is also a palace of transformation and healing. For example, let's say there is someone at work you cannot get along with, but you wish to change the situation for the better. Enter your sanctuary and in your imagination, invite your coworker to join you there. Become her friend, find out what is bothering her, cheer her up, share stories and jokes, have fun together. As you become good friends in your sanctuary, you will be amazed to find the same thing happening in real life.

Here's another example, if you are too shy, visit your sanctuary and populate it with people you would like to meet. Then in your imagination transform yourself into a confident person, and speak to everyone there.

Since this all occurs in your mind, there is nothing to fear. You can be as brave as you would like.

As you practice being the person you would like to be in your sanctuary, you will slowly change to that person in real life! Why is that? Well, when you practice visualization (also called imagery), you are speaking the language of the subconscious. Although our conscious or rational mind thinks in words, the language of the subconscious consists of images, feelings, and sensations. By practicing visualization and repeating your role-playing in your sanctuary, your subconscious will interpret and accept it as real life experience. In other words, you will be reprogramming your mind.

If you carefully follow the eight steps, by the time you enter your sanctuary, you will be in the alpha brain wave state. Another term to describe the state is hypnagogic or light hypnosis. So, with practice and experimentation, you will discover your retreat is a powerful tool that can bring about inner change.

34

Most Important

What is most important in life?

Although we may hesitate before arriving at the ONE most important thing in life, it is an easy matter to think of several things that are important to us. Some of the things that immediately come to mind are a job, money, friends, food and shelter, and a spouse and family. Now, we cannot get any of the above without the help of others. So, how do we get their help?

Life gives back to us what we give to it. So, if I help others, what do you suppose they will do? That's right, they will help me. Because we need the help of others to reach our goals, one of the most important things in life is TO HELP OTHERS, THEREBY RECEIVING THEIR HELP. But don't misunderstand. The purpose of helping others is not because we need their help, but because THEY NEED OUR HELP.

How do you feel when you are served by an ingratiating waiter in a restaurant? It is not pleasant when a waiter fawns on you because he wants a big tip. But when the waiter is sincere and offers impeccable service because he takes his job seriously, it is a delightful experience. For this simple reason, when we help others, SINCERITY and the DESIRE TO ALWAYS DO AND BE OUR BEST must be our guiding principles.

But what causes us to serve others with a pure motive? Isn't it LOVE? Now we can answer the question. The most important thing in life is LOVE because, as Marianne Williamson wrote in her book *"A Return to Love,"* LOVE IS OUR SOUL PURPOSE. Now that we know the answer, we can begin to reflect on the meaning of LOVE and the fruit it bears.

Love means to cherish, hold dear, and treasure. We do not hurt, harm, or cause pain to those we love; rather, we seek to relieve their suffering. Also, love is liberating because it is the absence of fear. It frees us from suspicion, hostility, envy, and resentment. It rejoices in the achievements of others. It is not about wanting people; it's about wanting people to be happy. It's not about wanting to possess or control others; it's about wanting to set them free.

Here is an excellent description of love by John Oxenham (real name: William Arthur Dunkerley, 1852 ~ 1941), "Love ever gives. Forgives, outlives. And ever stands with open hands. And while it lives, it gives. For this is love's prerogatives - to give, and give, and give." Love is all there is. What more do we need to know?

Before we can love others, we have to discover and experience it for ourselves. Although it is helpful to say we first need to love ourselves, it is also inaccurate to say so. You see, to love oneself implies two people: the lover and the beloved. But we are not two; we are one. So, it is more accurate to say that when we become still and plunge into our depths, we will discover that we ARE love. Love is our very nature. This becomes clear when we watch infants smile at strangers. Igor Stravinsky (1882 ~ 1971) said something similar, "Is it not by love alone that we succeed in penetrating to the very essence of being?"

Love is not about feeling good; it is about doing good. A perfect example of love in action is Mother Teresa (1910 ~ 1997). But how did such a tiny woman, barely five feet tall, find the energy to work so tirelessly? The answer can be found in the words of Thomas ã Kempis (1379 ~ 1471), "Love feels no burden, thinks nothing of trouble, attempts what is above its strength... It is therefore able to undertake all things, and it completes many things, and warrants them to take effect, where he who does not love would faint and lie down."

When we do all things with love, we infuse our tasks and ourselves with energy. Nevertheless, after considering the extraordinary hurdles overcome by Mother Teresa, we may feel painfully inadequate and doubt that we can make much of a difference. At such a time, we should earnestly listen to her own words: "Do not think that love in order to be genuine has to be extraordinary. What we need is to love without getting tired. Be faithful in small things because it is in them that your strength lies."

Mother Teresa also exemplified one of the fruits of love, which is RESPECT for others. When asked by a reporter if she tried to convert those she helped, she replied, "Of course I convert. I convert you to be a better Hindu or a better Muslim or a better Protestant. Once you've found God, it's up to you to decide how to worship him." It would bode well for us to follow her example, for if we cannot respect others, we cannot respect God.

Innately, we seek freedom, joy, and endless growth. They are the ingredients for happiness, and they are also the fruit of love. No longer a hostage of anger, a captive of greed, or a prisoner of negative thinking, love frees us to be ourselves. As to joy, it is the natural by-product of bringing joy to others. And for endless growth to flourish, we need an environment of love, for we cannot learn from those we don't love. Love allows us to accept others and makes us willing to listen to what they have to say, the reward of which is knowledge, learning, and growth.

"The essence of love is kindness," said Robert Louis Stevenson (1850 ~ 1894). Those who are portals of love are kind, gentle, and humble. They express their love by serving others, and their service provides meaning and purpose in their lives. On the physical plane, an enlarged heart is a malady, but spiritually, an enlarged heart embraces more and more of humanity, raising our consciousness. As our heart expands, we come to love everything under the sun: the streams, brooks, trees, and creatures of the forest. This leads us to God, for as Vincent Van Gogh (1853 ~ 1890) said, "The best way to know God is to love many things." When we love, we are not bringing God into our heart. Rather, we are stepping into the heart of God. What better way to get to know Him?

This is the time of year when we think of fireplaces, chimneys, and socks hung out for Santa to fill with presents. Yet, Frank Tebbets reminds us that "A life without love in it is like a heap of ashes upon a deserted hearth, with the fire dead, the laughter stilled and the light extinguished." To the deserted, the lonely, the impoverished, let's come bearing the gift of love. For as Oscar Wilde wrote, "Who, being loved, is poor?" I'm sure you agree with Euripides (480 ~ 406 BC) that "Love is all we have, the only way that each can help the other." Although this article has an ending, love does not. When we immerse ourselves in it, we get a taste of eternity. That's why Alfred Lord Tennyson (1808 ~ 1892) wrote, "...brief is life but love is long."

35

Most Important Goals

Slight not what's near while aiming at what's far

I know someone who feels guilty when he spends a good part of the day sitting on a park bench, soaking in the world of nature. He's equally uncomfortable about lying in bed for several hours while listening to classical music. Even when engaging in small talk with friends he's embarrassed. How can one feel guilty about enjoying life? Well, we have been brainwashed by society to believe that we are worthless unless we pursue a 'worthwhile' goal.

Yet, no goal is more worthwhile than the pursuit of your own happiness. You see, helping those in need may appear to be noble, but it's not a wise thing to do if it depresses you. After all, who wants to be helped by a gloomy, moody person? If you begrudgingly 'help' others, all you will succeed in is spreading more unhappiness. No, it is far better to look after your own contentment before considering the happiness of others. For when you allow yourself to be happy, you become a beacon, brightening the lives of everyone you meet.

After taking care of our own happiness, we can then branch out and start tackling some challenging goals. But here, too, be cautious. For although it will be necessary to focus on our goals before we can reach them, if we become too consumed by them, there is the danger of neglecting the present moment. We can become so wrapped up in the future that the present slips by unnoticed. Yet, it is only in the present that we are alive. The future is but a dream and the past, but a graveyard. We are here to experience life and add to it. But how can we add to it if we don't experience it?

Another pitfall of focusing on our goals too intently is that we may unwittingly extinguish spontaneity. By allowing ourselves to be blown about by the winds of the present moment, we experience the adventure of life, the unexpected, and the unplanned. When we willingly let go of the rigid confines of our goals, we can take part in the dance of life in which we neither try to control it nor try to be controlled by it. That is, we become dancing partners, not quite sure who is doing the leading.

To illustrate my point, let's look at the actions of two men. Ray and Ismail attended a seminar and developed interest in a book the speaker mentioned. After the seminar, Ray walked into a bookstore and asked for the book. In moments he had it and proudly left the store, marvelling at his efficiency and happy that he reached his goal.

Ismail also went to a bookstore. But once he found the book, he didn't stop there. He thought to himself, "Now that I'm here, I might as well browse." Ismail leisurely browsed with nothing specific in mind. He left himself open to whatever the present moment had in store for him. After a while, he came across a remarkable book, a work that had the potential to change his life. It dealt with a subject he never thought about. He smiled to himself as he realized that he never would have asked or searched for the book because it dealt with a subject new to him. Like Ray, Ismail achieved his goal, but by remaining in the present and leaving himself open to the unlimited possibilities that surrounded him, he accomplished a great deal more.

Ray focused on his goal and reached it. But he is oblivious to the great opportunity he lost. It may be years before he catches up to Ismail (if he ever catches up with him at all). Ismail, on the other hand, is more attuned to life. He understands the give and take. Through the practice of goal-setting, he guides life in bringing him the outcomes he wants. Yet, he remains balanced by spending just as much time open to the unexpected gifts that life brings.

Trying too hard to reach a goal can be a formula for failure. It is like the engine of your automobile freezing because of excessive heat. And it is what Émile Coué (1857 ~ 1926) called the "Law of Reversed Effect." This law did not escape the attention of one of the Rabbinic sages known as Rabbi Pinhas, for it is written in the Mishnah, "What you pursue, you don't get. But what you allow to grow slowly in its own way, comes to you." Besides, gritting one's teeth and trying with all one's might can be a source of stress. And stress depletes one's energy and clouds one's thinking, thereby lessening one's chances of success. So, this is another reason for loosening your grip on your goals and allowing life to play a part in deciding what you can do, be, and have.

True, goals are important in life. But we will become much more successful by delaying our personal goals until we have set the following ones as a foundation.

1. BALANCE is the ultimate goal. Don't be like Ray, so focused on your goal that you grow blind to the opportunities that surround you in the present. As Euripides (BCE 480 ~ 406) taught "Slight not what's near while aiming at what's far." Be cautious, for a life without balance is a life half lived.

2. Live with AWARENESS. "Life is denied by lack of attention, whether it be to cleaning windows or trying to write a masterpiece." (Nadia Boulanger, 1887 ~ 1979).

3. VISION. What is your reason for being or purpose? After you create your life purpose, you will be ready to work on your personal goals. For as Henry J. Golding wrote, "What our deepest self craves is not mere enjoyment, but some supreme purpose that will enlist all our powers and give unity and direction to our life."
4. Appreciation and GRATITUDE. He who appreciates what he has is rich; he who lives without gratitude is poor.
5. APPRECIATION OF WHAT IS. Don't merely appreciate what you HAVE, but appreciate what IS. When you learn to appreciate nature, art, beauty, music, poetry, literature, sculpture, painting, and photography, you will lead a joyful life.
6. Learn to THINK BEFORE YOU ACT. By controlling your emotions, you will retain the power of choice, which is the rudder that will guide your ship.
7. Personal GROWTH. Besides enjoying what IS, get excited about what CAN BE. This is the arena in which we strive to reach our potential and where we leave our mark on the world.

Here are some parting words given by Benjamin E. Mayes, "It must be borne in mind that the tragedy of life doesn't lie in not reaching your goal. The tragedy lies in having no goal to reach. It isn't a calamity to die with dreams unfulfilled, but it is a calamity not to dream. It is not a disaster to be unable to capture your ideal, but it is a disaster to have no ideal to capture. It is not a disgrace not to reach the stars, but it is a disgrace to have no stars to reach for. Not failure, but low aim is a sin."

Yes, reach for the stars, but while doing so, keep your feet firmly planted on the ground, and don't let your dreams of tomorrow veil the opportunities of today.

If you found this subject interesting and wish to get a different perspective on goal-setting, you will enjoy reading these two books: 1. *LIVING WITHOUT A GOAL, Finding the Freedom to Live a Creative and Innovative Life,* by James Ogilvy, Currency-Doubleday, 1995. 2. *GOAL-FREE LIVING: How to* Have *the Life You Want NOW!,* by Stephen M. Shapiro, ISBN: 0-471-77280-1, 2005.

36

Overcoming Bad Habits

A map doesn't take you where you want to go. It merely points the way. If you really have a destination in mind, you'll have to get off the couch, get in your car, turn on the ignition, and start driving. Books are maps, not solutions. What I'm writing is a map, not a solution. There is only one solution to your problems, and that is YOU. When you are ready to start your journey to a new, better you, pick a map, study the directions, and DO what is necessary to get there.

Our reader continues: "Self-help books aren't geared towards the people that can't find a way to help themselves."

What you really mean is "books aren't geared towards people who WON'T find a way to help themselves. You see, it is a DECISION we make. We either decide to help ourselves ("I WILL do whatever is necessary.") or we decide to become a victim ("I CAN'T do whatever is necessary."). Why would anyone want to become a victim? Well, in their mind, it is convenient. You don't have to do anything; after all, you're helpless. So, you just sit around and wait for someone or something to solve your problems. This type of thinking is akin to feeding crocodiles. I'm referring to something Ronald Reagan (1911 ~ 2004) said: "To sit back hoping that someday, some way, someone will make things right is to go on feeding the crocodile, hoping he will eat you last -- but eat you he will." Don't feed your problems, but face them, and do something about them.

Our reader goes on: "I'm not asking for a solution to all my problems. I realized that only I can do that after all the therapy. I would however, like to know what you have done to overcome laziness and what steps you took to become a more productive person."

You mention that you are undergoing therapy, so I'll share some views on that subject. The word "therapy" has its origin in Greek and means to heal or treat. That's what a knowledgeable therapist does. Good therapists treat their patients for a short time, enabling them to get on with their lives as soon as possible.

Suppose you were wounded and the doctor applied balm to your wounds. If your wounds weren't healing after treatment, the doctor would realize that something is wrong and would try another form of treatment. Yet, some patients see psychiatrists for long periods of time. Sometimes as long as 10, 15, or 20 years. Isn't that odd? If the patient isn't being healed, how can that be called therapy?

So, be forewarned. There is good therapy and poor therapy. An example of good therapy would be Rational Emotive Behavior Therapy (R.E.B.T.) or Cognitive Behavior Therapy (C.B.T.). Both forms of therapy recognize that our problems are caused not by external events, but by our internal beliefs, thoughts, and feelings. So treatment consists of teaching patients how to change their beliefs and thoughts. When patients do so, their feelings and behavior also change, empowering them to handle their own problems. You can learn more about the subject here:

While taking therapy, one of the dangers is some patients put their lives on hold. That is, instead of thinking, "I will start solving my problems NOW," they think, "My life will improve AFTER I'm cured." In other words, they use their therapy as another excuse for not changing ("I will change AFTER I get better.").

Morita Therapy and Acceptance and Commitment Therapy both address this problem. They both teach there is no need to wait until you understand the cause of your problem. There is no need to wait until you master an elaborate coping strategy. You can start right where you are today. You can accept your flaws, weaknesses, and problems. You can say to yourself, "Yes, I'm not perfect, but I'm not stupid either. I know I have problems. I know I have to change. I know what I need to do. So, I will begin taking action steps today. One baby step at a time. I will do something to improve every day, no matter how small the step. And as long as I persist, one step at a time, it is impossible to fail. So, I begin NOW."

You can also easily teach yourself Acceptance and Commitment Therapy (ACT).

In fact, this will be my suggestion to our reader. Please pick up a copy of Dr. Steven C. Hayes and Spencer Smith's workbook *"Get Out of Your Mind & Into Your Life, The New Acceptance and Commitment Therapy"* (New Harbinger Publications, 2005, ISBN 1-57224-425-9, US $19.95).

Morita Therapy (which is a mixture of Zen philosophy and Western Psychology) and ACT are firmly entrenched in reality. For example, it is well known that it takes EFFORT to achieve anything worthwhile. M.T. and ACT practitioners, and well-grounded people, ACCEPT that fact. They don't fight it. They don't resist. They don't run away from a little 'pain.' They focus on the prize and do whatever it takes to get it.

But some try to replace 'pain', discomfort, and effort with pleasure, such as food, drink, and TV. Now, here is the paradox. Those who seek a life of pleasure end up in pain, for by refusing to make the effort to succeed, they fail and experience regret, shame, and guilt. And those who willingly accept 'pain,' end up with pleasure. For what can be more pleasurable than achieving your goals and reaching your dreams? This being so, the effort needed to overcome challenges is the seed that contains our happiness, which is exactly what we are looking for! So it makes sense to embrace 'pain' ("no pain, no gain").

Regarding how I overcame laziness, it is not a matter of being lazy or productive. Rather, it is about having good or bad habits. You are not lazy; you just have a bad habit. As David Hasslehoff said, "If you stand still long enough, you'll get stuck." That's what happened to you. You stood still so long you got stuck. The cure, as suggested above, is to take small action steps every day.

If you're not impressed by what David Hasslehoff had to say, consider the words of Leonardo Da Vinci (1452 ~ 1519), "Iron rusts from disuse, stagnant water loses its purity and in cold weather becomes frozen; even so does inaction sap the vigors of the mind."

37

Nasty People

How should we deal with nasty people?

People are not only flowers; they are butterflies. When you brush them away, you are brushing away God. How can it be otherwise? For we are all children of the one Creator.

We make the greatest spiritual progress when we master the most difficult teachings. Perhaps no other teaching is as difficult to understand as Christ's "Turn the other cheek." Before I quote it, let me point out that if Shakespeare and Dr. Phil (McGraw) were to comment on the same subject, the effect would be different. When reading the words of Shakespeare, we may say, "That's a beautiful verse," yet, when reading Dr. Phil's comments, we are more apt to say, "Wow, that's profound and useful advice." The difference is easy to understand. After all, Shakespeare's writings are over 400 hundred years old, so they may appear formal and stilted. In contrast, Dr. Phil speaks and writes in a modern, down-to-earth, punchy style that grabs our attention. So, for you to grasp the full impact of Christ's teaching, I'm going to quote Professor Eugene Peterson's translation of the New Testament, which is called "The Message," or MSG for short. His translation is written in a "Dr. Phil" style. Here is how Christ answers the question on how to deal with nasty people.

"If someone slaps you in the face, stand there and take it. If someone grabs your shirt, gift-wrap your best coat and make a present of it. If someone takes unfair advantage of you, use the occasion to practice the servant life. No more tit-for-tat stuff. Live generously. Here is a simple rule of thumb for behavior: Ask yourself what you want people to do for you; then grab the initiative and do it for them!

If you only love the lovable, do you expect a pat on the back? Run-of-the-mill sinners do that. If you only help those who help you, do you expect a medal? Garden-variety sinners do that. If you only give for what you hope to get out of it, do you think that's charity? The stingiest of pawnbrokers does that. I tell you, love your enemies.

Help and give without expecting a return. You'll never - I promise - regret it. Live out this God-created identity the way our Father lives toward us, generously and graciously, even when we're at our worst. Our Father is kind; you be kind. Don't pick on people, jump on their failures, criticize their faults - unless, of course, you want the same treatment. Don't condemn those who are down; that hardness can boomerang. Be easy on people; you'll find life a lot easier." (Luke 6:29 ~ 6:37, MSG)

The teachings of Buddha are also difficult. Here is an example taken from Chapter One of the Dhammapada (teachings of Buddha):

"'Look how he abused me and beat me, How he threw me down and robbed me.' Live with such thoughts and you live in hate. 'Look how he abused me and beat me, How he threw me down and robbed me.' Abandon such thoughts, and live in love."

A disciple asked Buddha, "How can you forgive someone who robbed you?" "What would you have me do," answered Buddha, "should I also give the robber my remaining possession: my peace of mind?" When we hang on to hostility, anger, and discontent, we become thieves, robbing ourselves of happiness. I like the way Malachy McCourt expressed the same idea, "Resentment is like taking poison and waiting for the other person to die."

The love that Christ and Buddha talk about is unconditional. But the manner in which many of us express our love is conditional. It is based on the premise "If you behave the way I want you to, I will love you." The problem with such thinking is that if we cannot accept others as they are, we cannot accept ourselves as we are. When we condemn others because of their flaws, we unwittingly condemn ourselves because of our faults. So, unconditional love is not only the RIGHT way to act; it is the SMART way to act.

You see, our psychological well-being and peace of mind depend on us becoming vessels of unconditional love. It is our nature to love. When we become unable to love unconditionally because of distorted or judgmental thinking, we experience pain. Contrary to common belief, suffering is not caused by the fact that others do not love us. Rather, it is caused by the fact that we do not love others. Once we stop judging people, we'll be able to see the good they have to offer and we'll be able to return to our natural state of love.

Summing up, how do we deal with nasty people? We begin by awakening to the truth that there are no nasty people; there are just people. Some are asleep. Some are awake. Some are somewhere in-between. The question we need to ask ourselves is, "Which group am I in and what will I do about it?" Confucius (551 ~ 479 BC) tells us what we can do about it, "The rule of life is to be found within yourself. Ask yourself constantly, 'What is the right thing to do?'"

38

Nature of Life

Is life an adventure or misadventure?

Is life an adventure or a misadventure? The question is an important one because the view we take colors everything we experience. Our attitude or perspective either works for or against us. So, now and then we need to pause and examine which way our life is heading. After all, if we don't change our direction, we will end up where we are heading.

If we believe life is a misadventure or struggle, we live with resentment, distrust, and fear. We also feel that life is unfair, painful, and a form of punishment. Yet, our view of life is a choice we make. If we don't like what we see, we can change channels just the way we do on a TV set. Are you getting tired of seeing nothing but violence and suffering? Well, then, change channels! For a delightful change, take a look at all the good that is taking place in the world.

Remember that you can always choose what you decide to focus on. When we shift our focus from the negative to the positive, we begin to see the world in a new way. This change of perspective causes us to act differently. And by acting differently, life itself becomes different for us.

The secret of life is realizing that it is a great adventure. Missing this simple point can have disastrous effects. For example, imagine you and a stranger are strapped into a roller coaster. The stranger was plucked out of a primitive society and knows nothing about modern life. At the end of the ride, how will his experience differ from yours? In his eyes, the ride was a devilish form of torture. During the entire trip he was bewildered and in fear. And you? You enjoyed every thrilling moment!

Can you see how the failure to understand the nature of a roller coaster prevented the primitive native from enjoying the ride? It is no different with life. Those who have yet to learn that life is an adventure mistakenly believe they are victims of circumstances, condemned to a life of suffering.

Yet, once we understand the nature of life, everything changes. Can a roller coaster ride be exciting without steep falls and sharp twists and turns? Neither can life be exhilarating unless there are challenges to face, hurdles to surmount, and problems to solve. Adventurers understand that, so they don't fight and struggle with events, but choose to go with the flow. True, the flow may be as turbulent as white-water rafting, but isn't that part of the adventure?

Life invites us to become adventurers. It invites us to stop whining and start shinning, to stop being a victim and start being a victor. It invites us to journey on a quest to discover, uncover, and recover our potential. It invites us to become the hero in our life story by living courageously. It invites us to lead potent lives in which we make a difference by contributing and adding to life.

Life is not a war to wage, but a gift to cherish. We will realize this as soon as we change our focus from what we lack to what we have. Our feeling of gratitude and sense of appreciation releases energy, which will then help us to continue tirelessly in our adventure.

Adventurers don't repress or hide their emotions. Like rainbows, they burst into color as they feel and express a full range of feelings. Fear, anger, disgust, joy, pity, loneliness, surprise, elation, enthusiasm, passion, embarrassment, pain, sorrow, happiness, awe, calmness, and confusion are just a few of the emotions they experience. Unlike the numbness of the living dead, adventurers are alive with vibrant feelings. They feel life, soak it in, sense it, taste it, and fully express it.

Another characteristic of adventurers is their willingness to embrace change and uncertainty. And why shouldn't they? For change and uncertainty are just other words for surprise. No wonder adventurers believe life is a celebration; after all, they spend their entire lives in a surprise party.

They love dueling with the unexpected because it keeps them on their toes. Our lives don't have to be boring, they can be as exciting as that of any swashbuckler. All we have to do is accept life's offer; it's asking us to jump in and join in the fun. "The Big Question is," according to Joseph Campbell (1904 ~ 1987), "whether you are going to be able to say a hearty YES to your adventure."

If we're just neophyte wayfarers wanting to become heroic adventurers, how do we get from where we are to where we want to be? The best way to begin is with an inspiring dream. Pick a dream that is worthy of a hero. For as Renaissance man Robert Fritz wrote, "If you limit your choices only to what seems possible or reasonable, you disconnect yourself from what you truly want, and all that is left is compromise." When we live life as an adventure, our destination isn't as important as the transformation we undergo, so don't worry about whether you become entirely successful or not.

Another thing you can do is open your eyes and see. See what? See what Jawaharlal Nehru (1889 ~ 1964) spoke about,

"We live in a wonderful world that is full of beauty, charm and adventure. There is no end to the adventures that we can have if only we seek them with our eyes open." Every crossroad we come to is a choice between following the path of adventure or the road to misery. Which will it be? As long as we awaken from our slumber, and look for the right path, we will find it. When we open our hearts, minds, and eyes to what the world offers, we allow it to flood us with riches, so remain alert.

Also, to sustain our adventure, we need to make the right choices. For when we don't choose to befriend others, we choose to be lonely. When we don't choose to open our hearts to others, we choose to get nothing in return and turn our backs on opportunity. When we don't choose to elevate our thoughts, we contaminate our minds with stinking thinking. And if we don't choose to live in the present, we relinquish the only moment we are alive and have power.

You can add a great deal of pleasure to the adventure of life with some humor. For example, the renowned Radio Comic Fred A. Allen (1894 ~ 1957) had this to say, "Life, in my estimation, is a biological misadventure that we terminate on the shoulders of six strange men whose only objective is to make a hole in one with you." Despite the value of humor, I'll end on a serious note by quoting from the wisdom of Helen Keller (1880 ~ 1968), "Avoiding danger is no safer in the long run than outright exposure. Life is either a daring adventure or nothing. To keep our faces toward change and behave like free spirits in the presence of fate is strength undefeatable."

39

Negative Thinking

'Negativitis' cripples the human spirit

Does it seem strange that some people COMPLAIN they don't have enough TIME to be happy, yet they find enough time to be sad? Not really. You see, their deplorable plight has nothing to do with having sufficient or insufficient time. It has everything to do with complaining. After all, complaining is the negation of happiness. It's impossible to complain and be happy at the same time.

So, beware of that insidious disease known as 'negativitis' (negative thinking). It is as pervasive as the common cold, but far more damaging. It mutilates, cripples, and corrodes the human spirit. Those infected by it are broken men and women aimlessly plodding along. The dark clouds brooding over them obscure their vision and cause them to become confrontational, apathetic, and cynical. Their lives are like flat champagne, without any sizzle. So, how do we inoculate ourselves against such a harmful disease? It was only after learning about the horrible effects of smoking that people began to give it up. It may be wise to do the same here. So, let's review the effects of negativitis.

1. Complaining is worse than doing nothing, for it is digging the rut one is in deeper and deeper. Each time one complains, it becomes increasingly difficult to climb out of the ditch they've created. To loosen the grip of this vicious habit, we need to become aware of our complaining, stop it

in its tracks, and immediately look for something positive to say. It's just a matter of replacing a bad habit with a good one.

2. A negative attitude is self-defeating. We won't find solutions to life's problems by looking for someone or something to blame. Those who say, "Positive thinking doesn't work for me," have got it backwards. It's not positive thinking that has to work; YOU have to work. For example, you have to work at appreciating what you have instead of moaning about what you lack.
3. Failure to do what you want to do (be happy) causes physical and mental stress. A rotten attitude, not only delays success, but also shortens life by damaging the immune system (to learn more on how your thoughts affect your immune system, investigate psychoneuroimmunology). So, besides the diseases directly caused by stress, such as heart disease and ulcers, we become susceptible to all manner of other diseases because of a weakened immune system.
4. Do you know anyone with a negative attitude? How many years have they been that way? Two years? Five years? Ten years? That's how many years of happiness and success they have robbed themselves of. Blinded by their own negativity, they are prevented from seeing the good around them.
5. One characteristic of negative thinkers is their need to have the world behave according to their wishes. They have never grown up and still live with childish demands. Whenever people and the world fail to act according to their selfish wishes, they are unhappy. Such a poisonous attitude prevents them from growing and learning how to cope with life's challenges.
6. Everything negative we say about ourselves to ourselves (self-talk) and to others is a suggestion. We are unwittingly

practicing self-hypnosis, programing ourselves for failure, and creating self-fulfilling prophecies.

7. The negative world of our imagination creates a negative world that is real and one that we are forced to live in. Take Ralph, for example. He's always complaining about life. "Nowadays people are rude and surly. No matter where you go or what you do, you have to deal with ill-bred people." As he said this, we made our way to a coffee shop. Once inside, we were greeted by a cheerful chap who asked us what we would like. Sighing (as if it took a great effect to speak), Ralph, almost inaudibly, ordered a medium sized regular coffee. When it arrived, he started complaining. Pointing to the cup, he said, "This is medium?" Without waiting for a response, he added, "You should have told me your cups are so small; I would have ordered a large one if I knew." Despite the long line that Ralph was holding up, the man behind the counter tried to be patient. Without complaint, he took away the small coffee and replaced it with a large one. As soon as it arrived, Ralph looked at it aghast and bellowed, "You call this regular? There's not enough cream!" The man behind the counter, who only moments ago was cheerful was now upset and sarcastically replied, "Yes, for MOST people, this is regular, but if you INSIST, I'll put in more cream. Perhaps next time you may want to ask for DOUBLE cream!" I was next, so I got my coffee and joined Ralph at the table. "See," he told me, "what did I say to you? People are rude." Yes, in Ralph's world, people ARE rude, but what he does not realize is he makes them so.

8. A particularly pernicious effect of 'negativitis' is that it sets one up for the mentality of a victim. Those with a woe-is-me attitude sit around in misery, waiting to be rescued. But they

wait in vain because no one can rescue them from their own attitude. They are the only ones who can change it. And until they do so, they are condemned to continue suffering.

9. Another adverse effect of negativity is that it sets one up for the magic-bullet-syndrome. That is, the victims of 'negativitis' spends their time looking for a quick, easy fix, when none exists. By denying a fundamental law of life that states anything worthwhile requires effort to achieve, they achieve nothing. They won't make progress until they realize that nothing in life is free. They've got to be willing to do what it takes to get what they want.
10. Also, beware of the fact that negative people attract other complainers. Because those who live in a world of doom and gloom alienate others, they have no choice but to look for other negative people to associate with. They then feed off one another and get locked in a clique of losers.
11. The constant stress that flows from a negative attitude also saps one's energy, focus, and motivation. It is hardly a formula for success.
12. Also of great concern is the fact that those who refuse to work on improving their negative attitude may slide into depression, self-pity, and hopelessness.
13. Additionally, negative people not only harm themselves; they harm the world. They cease to make a contribution to it. Instead of helping, they spread gloom and misery everywhere. If they insist on infecting others, why not infect them with laughter? If they must carry something contagious, why not carry a smile?

Imagine being in a small boat drifting in a river. And imagine being unaware that your boat has a motor. As long as you fail to use that motor you will be a captive of the river. You will be a prisoner without any control over your destination. Yet, the boat that we're in does have a motor. We can use it to change course. That motor is our power of choice. All we have to do is choose to look for the good, for when we do so, that is all we will find!

40

Never Too Late

It is never too late to be what you might have been

Is it really true that you're never too old to start a new career or make a dramatic change in your life? What if you're 72, or 82? Isn't that too old to learn a new language? Not so. Two thousand years ago, the Roman Statesman, Cato, learned Greek at age 80.

Can you be creative in old age? How about Goethe? His greatest Work, 'Faust' wasn't completed until he was 80. And Michelangelo was 71 when he painted the Sistine Chapel.

More examples? Luigi Cornaro, a Venetian scholar, started writing on geriatrics at the age of 83. His classic treatise 'The Joys of Old Age' was written in 1562 when he was 95. In modern times, the great philosopher, mathematician, and pacifist, Bertrand Russell, participated and was arrested in an antinuclear demonstration when he was 89.

We mustn't forget about Grandma Moses, who started painting at 80. Did you know twenty-five percent of her more than 1,500 paintings were done after she was one hundred?

When I was a high school student, Henry Little, the president of The Institution for Savings in Newburyport, Massachusetts, decided to retire so a younger man could take over. Mr. Little retired when he was 102. The younger man who took over was 83.

Little Lessons

What can we learn from the above examples? They were all passionate about what they were doing. Passion is a source of energy and youthfulness, for as Benjamin Franklin wrote, "Those who love deeply never grow old; they may die of old age, but they die young."

Also, they realized it is far better to be 70 years young than 40 years old, so they didn't let their age stop them from chasing their dream. They understood that it is never too late to do something, and the time for action is now. Unlike King Richard II, they never lamented, "I wasted time, and now doth time waste me."

Another lesson is when opportunities appeared, they took the plunge. Yes, there were risks involved, but why be afraid of life? Death, maybe, but not life. Rita Coolidge appreciated how important throwing caution to the wind is when she said, "Too often the opportunity knocks, but by the time you push back the chain, push back the bolt, unhook the locks and shut off the burglar alarm, it's too late."

In my own case, the elixir of youth is my daily dose of new experiences and knowledge. Apparently Henry Ford felt in a similar fashion, for he said, "Anyone who stops learning is old, whether this happens at twenty or eighty. Anyone who keeps on learning not only remains young but becomes constantly more valuable, regardless of physical capacity."

Finally, here is an Arabic saying to mull over, "When you see old people amiable, mild, equable, content, and good-humored, be sure that in their youth they have been just, generous, and forbearing. In their end they do not lament the past, nor dread the future; they are like the evening of a fine day."

Poem by Edward Tuck

Age is a quality of the mind:
If you have left your dreams behind,
If hope is cold;
If you no longer look ahead,
If your ambition's fires are dead—
Then you are old.
But if from life you take the best,
And if in life you keep the jest,
If love you hold;
No matter how the years go by,
No matter how the birthdays fly—
You are not old.

41

New Awakening

Awakening from our slumber because of a shock

Sometimes it takes a shock to bring us to our senses. Catastrophic news can jar us from our slumber and cause us to reconsider how we are leading our lives. Consider Tim, for instance. Imagine his shock when told by his doctor he had a terminal illness (cancer) and should prepare for death. His initial shock was followed by anger. Interestingly, he changed that anger into a fierce determination to prove the doctors were wrong. Like Marcel Proust (1871 ~ 1922), Tim believed "For each illness that doctors cure with medicine, they provoke ten in healthy people by inoculating them with the virus that is a thousand times more powerful than any microbe: the idea that one is ill." Tim also took to heart the advice that appears in a Mother Goose rhyme, "For every ailment under the sun, There is a remedy, or there is none, If there be one, try to find it; If there be none, never mind it."

Tim refused to buy into the idea that he was ill. He ignored all dire warnings to prepare for death and just went on living. And that was more than seven years ago! Not only did Tim get a reprieve from death, but he also got an opportunity to reflect on what is most important in life for him. There is nothing like a death sentence to help us set our priorities.

If you discovered you had a terminal illness, would you do anything differently? Most of us would. Now, here's the point:

you DO have a terminal illness. All of us do. It is called LIFE. So, what are we waiting for? The time to do things differently, set our priorities, and strive toward our goals is now. We can no longer wait. We cannot afford to treat life like a rainstorm, whiling away the time as we wait for it to stop. When will we start to spend time on what we believe is most important in our lives? The choice we have to make is a simple, but urgent one. For as Time Management Expert Alan Lakein says, "Time = Life, Therefore, waste your time and waste your life, or master your time and master your life." To reinforce this message, I'm including a list of reasons to act on our priorities now.

1. Because of the brevity of life, there is no time to delay. Yang Chu (Yang Zhu, 440 ~ 360 BC?) elegantly reminds us how brief life is, "One hundred years is the limit of a long life. Not one in a thousand ever attains to it. Yet if they do, still unconscious infancy and old age take up about half this time. The time he passes unconsciously while asleep at night, and that which is wasted though awake during the day, also amounts to another half of the rest. Again pain and sickness, sorrow and fear, fill up about a half, so that he really gets only ten years or so for his enjoyment. And even then there is not one hour free from some anxiety." Here's how Austin Dobson (1840 ~ 1921) expresses his view on the subject, "Time goes, you say? Ah, no! Alas, time stays, we go."
2. The sooner we act, the sooner we can learn from our experience, make corrections, and reap the rewards. Remember, things generally take longer to do than we imagine, and we may not get it right the first time. We cannot choose the day and time we will be successful, but we can choose to begin now, thereby hastening our eventual success.

3. Although everything takes longer to do than imagined, they are also easier to do than imagined. But this advantage disappears if we keep postponing things. For as we delay, the number of tasks keeps rising, reducing the time we have to spend on our projects. As we try to cram many tasks into the little time we have, the quality of our effort decreases and the likelihood of making a mistake rises.
4. The need to act now should be a foregone conclusion, for the only time we have the power to act is at this very moment. The past and present cannot help us, only this moment can.
5. The consequences of our positive actions boost our value, confidence, knowledge, and power. What better time to enjoy these benefits than now?
6. Enjoy life instead of watching others do so. Become a participant, not a spectator. Rather than watching what happens to you, make what you want to happen, happen. If we have time to complain about how bad things are, we have time to do something about it. Keep in mind what Andy Warhol (1928? ~ 1987) said, "They always say that time changes things, but you actually have to change them yourself."
7. Self-discovery. Surprise yourself by becoming the person you never dreamed possible. For as Golo Mann (1909 ~ 1994, the third son of Thomas Mann) said, "Man is always more than he can know of himself; consequently, his accomplishments, time and again, will come as a surprise to him."
8. Do you have any regrets about time you have wasted? If so, use those regrets as a catalyst to take advantage of your remaining time to reach your goals. By sticking to your priorities, you will protect yourself from future regrets over what might have been.

9. Awaken to opportunity, for opportunities come to those that act. And once it appears, we need to act quickly because it may never return. The news of the death of a loved one, for example, may arrive before that phone call we were planning to make to them. Opportunities don't linger. They are like worms that are gobbled up by early birds.
10. If we keep ourselves busy, there will be no time to complain or fall under the negative influences of others. Many a person avoided disaster by keeping busy.
11. Create more time! If we always tackle our tasks as soon as they appear, we act efficiently and wind up with more time to spend as we please. I look at it this way, procrastination is a life extinction plan while a constant stream of action is a life extension plan.
12. Experience peace of mind. We may not be able to do everything we would like to each day, but if we at least finish what is most important, we will be able to sleep soundly.

When are we going to act? Today! Why are we going to act today? Kalidasa, the 5th century AD, Indian Sanskrit poet explains, "Look to this day for it is life. In its brief course lie all the realities and verities of existence, the bliss of growth, the splendor of action, the glory of power. For yesterday is but a dream, and tomorrow is only a vision, but today, well lived, makes yesterday a dream of happiness and every tomorrow a vision of hope. Look well, therefore to this day."

42

New Ideas

I had a monumental idea this morning, but I didn't like it (Samuel Goldwyn)

Ideas, like the air we breathe, are omnipresent. And they are to the mind what light is to the eyes. Everywhere you go and every act you do provides opportunities for useful ideas. Every time you turn on the radio or TV, flip through the pages of your favorite newspaper, magazine or book, ideas are there, waiting to be picked. The moments spent waiting in the doctor or dentist's office and the time spent commuting or computing can be opportunities to garner new ideas. At the same time you're cooking dinner, you can also be cooking up fresh ideas. The point is to be aware of the ever-present opportunities.

Great ideas inspire, instruct, guide, and lead us. They are treasures that enrich our lives. They provide different viewpoints, a basis of comparison, and clarity of vision. "A pile of rocks ceases to be rocks when somebody contemplates it with the idea of a cathedral in mind." (Antoine De Saint-Exupery, 1900 ~ 1944) Ideas are storehouses of power. Witness the freedom fighters or terrorists that willingly give their lives for an idea. Our minds expand in direct proportion to the number and size of the ideas we embrace. The ultimate idea is the cosmos we live in, which is a reflection of the grandeur of the mind that created it.

The Founder of USA Today, Al Neuharth, said, "Never hesitate to steal a good idea." But don't steal it. Rather, embrace it. Mull it over. Pick it apart and make it your own. That's precisely what every great thinker does. No one originates ideas, but merely refines and reshapes the ideas of others. All ideas are a collaborate effort. So, they are meant to be shared. Yet, when expressing our ideas, we usually do not transfer them to others as much as awaken those already lying dormant in their minds. This is enough of an introduction to the world of ideas and their value. Now, let's consider how to increase the harvest of our own ideas, thereby further improving our lives.

1. Realize that the midwives of good ideas are looking, listening, searching, questioning, and pondering. Always be on the alert for hidden treasure. Remain curious. There must be another way, a better way, or an easier way. Look for it and find it.
2. Fortunately, Samuel Goldwyn did not ignore every monumental idea he had. Likewise, don't ignore yours. On the contrary, always be prepared to record them. Keep an idea notebook handy. Like butterflies, ideas don't remain where they settle very long. They are fleeting. Capture them while the opportunity is there. And since they may appear at the most unexpected times, always be ready.
3. No matter how grand or noble our ideas are, they are pointless unless acted upon. The difference between a pile of rocks and a cathedral is the action we take to bring our idea to life. Some people have ideas; others put them to work. Ideas won't work unless we do. The value of action cannot be stressed too greatly. For sometimes it is action that generates the idea. For example, if I am smashing rocks, rather than sleeping under a tree, the thought may occur to me that the rocks could be used to build a cathedral.

4. Both Thomas A. Edison (1847 ~ 1931) and two time winner of the Nobel Peace Prize, Linus Pauling (1901 ~ 1994) agree that the best way to arrive at a brilliant idea is to have many. For the more ideas we generate, the greater our likelihood of coming up with a great one.
5. There are at least three levels of ideas: common ones, valuable insight, and breathtaking revelation. Pondering the first leads to the last. That is, don't merely have an idea, but scrutinize it; tear it apart. Question it. Challenge it. It has to be grappled before it can be assimilated. The more you investigate it, the deeper you probe, the greater your chances of striking gold. The Russian mystic Madame Swetchine (1782 ~ 1857) put it this way, "To have ideas is to gather flowers; to think, is to weave them into garlands."
6. Others won't accept your ideas until they accept you. But don't be guilty of making the same mistake. A diamond caked in mud is still a diamond. Never judge another. Anyone can share pearls of wisdom. Don't let prejudices prevent you from benefiting by them. Always remain open to the ideas of others, and remember that bright ideas often camouflage themselves as stupid ones.
7. Not every idea is worthwhile. The value of an idea is measured by the consequences it produces when acted upon. Cherish ideas that improve your life and scrap those that hinder it. Be open-minded, but not gullible. Beware of those who use the power of ideas to confuse, twist, and control the minds of others. It is important to realize that there are bad ideas as well as good ideas. Until we accept this fact, it will be difficult to distinguish between the two. We will become as immense or small as our ideas, so choose them carefully.

8. Learn how to break rules. Rules are helpful guides, but their restrictiveness can leave us in a rut. Challenge the validity of rules.
9. Be like children: learn to substitute what is needed for what is available. If a toy car is unavailable, the imagination of a child will allow a spool of thread to take its place. Try to discover how to get what you lack but wish to have. But when it is impossible to have what you want, find a replacement.
10. Learn how to combine the ideas of others with your own. What part of their idea is helpful for you to copy or adapt?
11. Don't be like people who treat new ideas like mosquitoes by brushing them aside or squeezing the life out of them. True, we become set in our ways and sheer force of habit makes change difficult. But growth is impossible without change, so don't resist it. Leaders are those who deliberately look for new ideas and adapt to them. Whether you are a leader or not is not dependent upon a title given to you, but upon the actions you take. Act like a leader and you will be one.
12. Don't let the criticism, frowns, and doubts of others squelch your ideas. Every new idea is first met with scorn. If you have a good idea and remain persistent, eventually it will be adopted by all.
13. Treasure new ideas, for once we gain new insight, we never see the world the same way. To expand your horizon and elevate your consciousness, all you have to do is be receptive. Reach out and embrace the ideas that surround you and are ignored by others.

43

No Time to Delay

Awakening from our slumber because of a shock

Sometimes it takes a shock to bring us to our senses. Catastrophic news can jar us from our slumber and cause us to reconsider how we are leading our lives. Consider Tim, for instance. Imagine his shock when told by his doctor he had a terminal illness (cancer) and should prepare for death. His initial shock was followed by anger. Interestingly, he changed that anger into a fierce determination to prove the doctors were wrong. Like Marcel Proust

(1871 ~ 1922), Tim believed "For each illness that doctors cure with medicine, they provoke ten in healthy people by inoculating them with the virus that is a thousand times more powerful than any microbe: the idea that one is ill." Tim also took to heart the advice that appears in a Mother Goose rhyme, "For every ailment under the sun, There is a remedy, or there is none, If there be one, try to find it; If there be none, never mind it."

Tim refused to buy into the idea that he was ill. He ignored all dire warnings to prepare for death and just went on living. And that was more than seven years ago! Not only did Tim get a reprieve from death, but he also got an opportunity to reflect on what was most important in life for him. There is nothing like a death sentence to help us set our priorities.

If you discovered you had a terminal illness, would you do anything differently? Most of us would. Now, here's the point: you DO have a terminal illness. All of us do. It is called LIFE. So, what are we waiting for? The time to do things differently, set our priorities, and strive toward our goals is now. We can no longer wait. We cannot afford to treat life like a rainstorm, whiling away the time as we wait for it to stop. When will we start to spend time on what we believe is most important in our lives? The choice we have to make is a simple, but urgent one. For as Time Management Expert Alan Lakein says, "Time = Life, Therefore, waste your time and waste your life, or master your time and master your life." To reinforce this message, I'm including a list of reasons to act on our priorities now.

1. Because of the brevity of life, there is no time to delay. Yang Chu (Yang Zhu, 440 ~ 360 BC) elegantly reminds us how brief life is, "One hundred years is the limit of a long life. Not one in a thousand ever attains to it. Yet if they do, still unconscious infancy and old age take up about half this time. The time he passes unconsciously while asleep at night, and that which is wasted though awake during the day, also amounts to another half of the rest. Again pain and sickness, sorrow and fear, fill up about a half, so that he really gets only ten years or so for his enjoyment. And even then there is not one hour free from some anxiety." Here's how Austin Dobson (1840 ~ 1921) expresses his view on the subject, "Time goes, you say? Ah, no! Alas, time stays, we go."
2. The sooner we act, the sooner we can learn from our experience, make corrections, and reap the rewards. Remember, things generally take longer to do than we imagine, and we may not get it right the first time. We cannot choose the day and time we will be successful, but we can choose to begin now, thereby hastening our eventual success.

3. Although everything takes longer to do than imagined, they are also easier to do than imagined. But this advantage disappears if we keep postponing things. For as we delay, the number of tasks keeps rising, reducing the time we have to spend on our projects. As we try to cram many tasks into the little time we have, the quality of our effort decreases and the likelihood of making a mistake rises.
4. The need to act now should be a foregone conclusion, for the only time we have the power to act is at this very moment. The past and present cannot help us, only this moment can.
5. The consequences of our positive actions boost our value, confidence, knowledge, and power. What better time to enjoy these benefits than now?
6. Enjoy life instead of watching others do so. Become a participant, not a spectator. Rather than watching what happens to you, make what you want to happen, happen. If we have time to complain about how bad things are, we have time to do something about it. Keep in mind what Andy Warhol (1928? ~ 1987) said, "They always say that time changes things, but you actually have to change them yourself."
7. Self-discovery. Surprise yourself by becoming the person you never dreamed possible. For as Golo Mann (1909 ~ 1994, the third son of Thomas Mann) said, "Man is always more than he can know of himself; consequently, his accomplishments, time and again, will come as a surprise to him."
8. Do you have any regrets about time you have wasted? If so, use those regrets as a catalyst to take advantage of your remaining time to reach your goals. By sticking to your priorities, you will protect yourself from future regrets over what might have been.

9. Awaken to opportunity, for opportunities come to those that act. And once it appears, we need to act quickly because it may never return. The news of the death of a loved one, for example, may arrive before that phone call we were planning to make to them. Opportunities don't linger. They are like worms that are gobbled up by early birds.
10. If we keep ourselves busy, there will be no time to complain or fall under the negative influences of others. Many a person avoided disaster by keeping busy.
11. Create more time! If we always tackle our tasks as soon as they appear, we act efficiently and wind up with more time to spend as we please. I look at it this way, procrastination is a life extinction plan while a constant stream of action is a life extension plan.
12. Experience peace of mind. We may not be able to do everything we would like to each day, but if we at least finish what is most important, we will be able to sleep soundly.

When are we going to act? Today! Why are we going to act today? Kalidasa, the 5th century AD, Indian Sanskrit poet explains, "Look to this day for it is life. In its brief course lie all the realities and verities of existence, the bliss of growth, the splendor of action, the glory of power. For yesterday is but a dream, and tomorrow is only a vision, but today, well lived, makes yesterday a dream of happiness and every tomorrow a vision of hope. Look well, therefore to this day."

44

Overcoming Adversity

Adversity: Here to Break Us or Make Us?

Pain, suffering, stress, and other difficulties are the admission tickets to the game of life. But, at times, we cannot help suspecting that life would be much more pleasant without the hassles. Is that what you think? Before answering, ponder the following. In a world without hurdles, there are no champions; without suffering, there are no saints; without battles, there are no victories; without rain, no rainbows. Doesn't it appear that a world that includes pain is more rewarding than one that doesn't? Isn't heat necessary to produce gold, pressure and polishing necessary to produce diamonds, and adversity necessary to produce character?

Here's how Henry Ford expressed the same sentiment: "Life is a series of experiences, each one of which makes us bigger, even though sometimes it is hard to realize this. For the world was built to develop character, and we must learn that the setbacks and grieves which we endure help us in our marching onward."

Points to Consider

1. Adversity is unavoidable. So, don't fight it, accept it. Develop the proper attitude, for as Havelock Ellis wrote, "Pain and death are part of life. To reject them is to reject life itself." Although pain is inevitable, suffering is optional. We

can choose to be strong. It is not misfortune that produces suffering, but an improper reaction to it.

Even under the worst circumstances, we can choose to focus on the positive rather than the negative. Thomas A. Edison is an example. In 1914, a fire almost destroyed his New Jersey laboratories. Valuable records of his experiments and two million dollars worth of equipment were lost. When surveying the damage, the sixty-seven year old Edison said, "There is great value in disaster. All our mistakes are burned up. Thank God we can start anew."

When Hurricane Mitch swept across Central America and parts of the U.S., it left a path of destroyed homes, dashed dreams, and broken hearts. After the storm subsided, birds returned to uprooted trees and began to sing. Isn't it true, as Rose F. Kennedy says, "Birds sing after a storm; why shouldn't people feel as free to delight in whatever remains to them?"

2. Realize that misfortune tells what fortune is. We need winter to appreciate spring, rain to appreciate the sunshine, and adversity to be thankful for the calm after the storm.

3. Recognize misfortune for what it is: an opportunity to lift yourself to a higher level. Sailors caught in a storm should pray not for safety from danger, but for deliverance from fear. Why should they accept the storm? Because a smooth sea never made a skillful mariner.

   When an eagle believes her eaglets are large enough to learn how to fly, she begins to take apart the nest and push the eaglets out. After this rude awakening, the eaglets discover they have wings! They can fly! The universe is constantly nudging us, pushing us off one cliff after another, in the hope that one day we, too, will discover our wings and soar to new heights.

4. Lessen your suffering by refusing to linger on past difficulties or expecting future ones. Problems of the present are difficult enough to deal with. Don't add to your misery by regretting the past or worrying about what might happen in the future. Mark Twain understood that it was pointless to fret about the future when he said, "I am an old man and have known a great many troubles, but most of them never happened."
5. Realize it could be worse. Count your blessings. Keep in mind the Persian proverb: I cried because I had no shoes until I saw someone with no feet.

Regardless of how horrible your circumstances, you are probably not paralyzed and unable to speak. However, Mr. Washington Roebling was. You see, more than 100 years ago, Washington's father, John, had a dream to build The Brooklyn Bridge. Experts at the time believed it to be impossible, but John finally persuaded the city to support his project. He and his son, Washington, were the lead engineers and the only ones who knew how to build such a bridge. After just a few months into the project, there was an accident that took the life of John and left his son with permanent brain damage. Although unable to speak, write, or walk, Washington's mind was alert and he could move one finger. Determined to realize his father's dream, he developed a code, which made it possible to communicate with his wife by tapping on her arm with his finger. Washington tapped on his wife's arm for thirteen years, relaying all the instructions for the engineers. Today, the bridge stands as a testimony of how we can overcome any obstacle, if only we choose to do so.

45

Overcoming Envy

Envy Shoots at Others, But Wounds Herself

Envy is pervasive and, therefore, makes an excellent topic. Even though it is widespread, however, the degree to which it is troubling varies from person to person. Yet, there is good reason to try to remove it from our lives, for envy is a thief that robs us of happiness. Or, as Buddha put it, "He who envies others does not obtain peace of mind."

Besides robbing us of happiness, envy also prevents us from enjoying what we already have. Worse than that is the physical damage done to our bodies by the toxic emotions of envy, resentment, and frustration. By the way, the knowledge that negative emotions have an adverse effect on our body is hardly new. For even the Old Testament teaches, "Envy and wrath shorten the life." (Ecclesiastes, 30:24)

Even if you were to think of envy as a trifling matter, at times the smallest of concerns can lead to huge problems if we do not nip it in the bud. For this reason, the British Cleric, Poet, and Mystic Thomas Traherne (1636 ~ 1674) wrote, "A little grit in the eye destroyeth the sight of the very heavens, and a little malice or ENVY a world of joys. One wry principle in the mind is of infinite consequence."

When his family was well-off, our reader felt comfortable among his wealthy friends. But after his family's finances fell, he felt that life was unfair. He wondered why this was happening to him and not his friends. After all, he was just as deserving, if not more so. Therefore, he grew resentful.

Why did this happen to our reader? Probably because life had better plans for him. You see, when everything is handed to us on a silver platter, we are denied the exhilaration and joy that follows success after a long struggle. True, if we inherit great wealth, we can spend it on various pleasures, but how short-lived they are! How shallow they are! Unless we struggle for our success, we will never know what it means to live a thrilling adventure, which is what life was meant to be.

The moral for our reader is embrace your turn of fortune. Delight in the knowledge that it represents an opportunity for you to reach undreamed of heights. You were placed on earth to live as a hero, not a beggar. Besides, why do you want to be like your friends? Greatness lies in following your own path. Strive for uniqueness, not conformity. The paradox is that often having less is having more. For when we have less wealth, we often have more drive, more ambition, more direction, more purpose, and more adventure.

Also, please understand there is a great difference between those who have had wealth handed to them and those who have had to work hard for their success. The difference is the former can lose everything they have, for all they have is wealth. But if the latter lose their wealth, they still have the skills and knowledge they got during their struggles. Armed with know-how and the scars to prove they can overcome obstacles, they have the resilience to bounce back after a so-called disaster. They are true survivors, for it is not wealth that provides security, but resilience.

It also needs to be said that envy is ignorance of the problems that others have. Your friends may be unhappy, have relationship problems, be ill, worried about the future, be bored, feel lost, be unsure of themselves, or have any number of a host of other problems. It is only your ignorance of their complaints that makes you envy them.

Additionally, you seem to be confused about the true nature of wealth. Wealth is freedom from want. By "freedom from want," I don't mean freedom from a lack of possessions, but freedom from a NEED for possessions. What you, your friends, and I really want is happiness. Constantly bombarded by commercials, however, we are often led astray, believing the next great product will bring happiness.

But, alas, happiness does not come from HAVING more, but from BEING more. Being MORE cooperative, helpful, encouraging, accepting, patient, understanding, trusting, supportive, compassionate, forgiving, cheerful, and caring. This form of behaviour is aligned with our true nature, so when we act that way, we feel good and discover what it is like to have heaven on earth. Moreover, when we wish others well and celebrate their successes, we uplift ourselves and destroy any remnants of envy.

In the second paragraph, our reader writes, "for some reason I keep focusing on what I don't have." His behavior doesn't stem from some mysterious reason; it's simply based on force of habit. So, it's time to change the habit. It's simple to do. Just start each day by writing the following questions and answering them in a journal: "What am I grateful for today? What am I excited about today? What am I looking forward to today?"

Answering these questions keeps you focused on the positive, energizes you, and jump-starts your day. Repeat this daily, and in a short time, you'll begin to see life in a new way. Much has been written about the importance of gratitude and I'm sure you KNOW all about that, but now it's time for you to FEEL it.

For a book you may find helpful, see *"LAW OF ATTRACTION: The Science of Attracting More of What You Want and Less of What You Don't"* by Michael J. Losier, Wellness Central, 2007. This book is less metaphysical and much more down-to-earth and practical than other books on the same subject.

46

Overcoming Failure

Failure is Nothing to Fear

Failure and Courage

Failure can be a beautiful experience. Why? Because it provides us with an opportunity to develop courage. Or, as Confucius said, "Our greatest glory is not in never falling, but in rising every time we fall." Anyone who has seen the movie Rocky can never forget the scene in which he continually rises after being knocked down in the ring over and over again. Bloodied and barely able to see, he continues to get up and stagger toward his opponent, while his manager shouts, "Rocky, stay down! Stay down!"

At one time we were all just like Rocky. As infants learning to walk we would just get up after each fall. We were courageous! What happened? Why did many of us change? Well, as infants, our parents encouraged us. That is, they brought out the courage that naturally resided in us. But as we grew and experienced the jeers instead of cheers of our peers, courage somehow got pushed into a corner of our psyche, and eventually we forgot ever having it.

It's time to say: I won't take it any more; I'm going to reclaim my courage! The best way to begin is by realizing that failure is an event, not a person. In other words, if you were to try something new and fail 18 times in a row, you would not be a

FAILURE, but a PERSON who has experienced 18 failures. That's a big difference. So, if there's something you want to do and are unsuccessful, dust yourself off and try again! Remember, the only people who never fail are those who never try.

Success Means Never Giving Up

What did Thomas A. Edison say after 10,000 unsuccessful attempts to develop his electric light bulb? He said, "I have not failed. I've just found 10,000 ways that won't work." Edison realized that men do not fail; they give up trying. He realized that success means not giving up. Shouldn't we be following his example?

Failure is more than an opportunity to develop courage. It is also a valuable lesson. When we learn from our mistakes, we can avoid committing them again. Besides, to succeed in life we need experience, and we gain experience by making mistakes. Don't be disheartened by failures; after all, you don't drown by falling in water; you drown by staying there.

Before a missile can hit its target, it needs feedback. Each moment it drifts from the target, the missile detects the error and adjusts its path to realign with its destination. It continues to do so until the moment of impact. Failure is also feedback. It is a reminder that we must take corrective action before we can reach our goal.

We can rejoice in our failures because each one brings us that much closer to success. The great Babe Ruth put it this way, "Every strike brings me closer to the next home run." Also, here's what Thomas J. Watson, founder of IBM, had to say on the subject, "Would you like me to give you a formula for... success? It's quite simple, really. Double your rate of failure. You're thinking of failure as the enemy of success. But it isn't at all... you can be discouraged by failure -- or you can learn from it. So go ahead and make mistakes. Make all you can. Because, remember that's where you'll find success."

Which is better, to try something and fail or to try nothing and succeed? I think you will agree it is far better to try. Remember, there are three kinds of people: those who make it happen, those who watch it happen, and those who say, "What happened?" If we wish to belong to the first group, we have to take risks and try. So, let's start today by defying failure, learning from our mistakes, and forging ahead.

47

Overcoming Fear of Death

The Fear of Death is Worse than Death

How can we reduce the negative impact of the fear of death? The best way I know of is to live with no regrets. I'll let Elizabeth Kübler-Ross (1926 ~ 2004) explain what I mean, "It is those who have not really lived -- who have left issues unsettled, dreams unfulfilled, hopes shattered, and who have let the real things in life (loving and being loved by others, contributing in a positive way to other people's happiness and welfare, finding out what things are REALLY you) pass them by -- who are most reluctant to die." (Sorry for the complexity of the sentence, but it's worthwhile struggling through it.)

Elizabeth Kübler-Ross was a pioneer in Thanatology (the study of the effects of death and dying), and she taught us the stages we go through as we face our own death. She originally gave five stages, which were later increased to seven. Not everyone goes through all the stages, nor do we necessarily go through the stages in the order shown below.

STAGES OF DEATH

Shock Stage: "Oh, my God!"
Denial Stage: "It can't be true!"
Anger Stage: "Why me?"
Bargaining Stage: "Spare me, God, and I will do something for You."

Depression Stage: "It's all over. I have nothing to look forward to."
Testing Stage: "What can I do to make my remaining days worthwhile?"
Acceptance Stage: "It doesn't make sense to fight the inevitable."

Of course, we don't want to become like Tony, immobilized by the fear of death. But neither should we want to remove the thought of our own death from our consciousness. On the contrary, if we wish to get the most out of life, we should heighten our Personal Death Awareness (PDA). The classic reference on this subject is "*PDA -- Personal Death Awareness*" by J. William Worden, Ph.D., Prentice-Hall, 1976 (ISBN: 0136572138). Another excellent book is *FACING DEATH, EMBRACING LIFE; Understanding What Dying People Want*, David Kuhl, M.D., Doubleday Canada, 2006. Although this book was written for terminal illness patients, we can all benefit from it because we are all dying of a terminal illness. (In our case, the name of the illness is LIFE.)

Although we are aware that others will die, we seldom think about our own death. That's what PDA refers to. It is about the awareness and contemplation of our own death. Here are some ways in which a higher PDA can improve our lives:

1. It is foremost an opportunity to live courageously. The higher our PDA, the more exhilaration, zest, and aliveness we experience. For it is in its contrast to death that life becomes infused with excitement, adventure, and pleasure. By remaining aware of our mortality, we stay connected to life.

2. The awareness of our own demise also serves as a reminder to enjoy the banquet of life. For as Omar Khayyam (1048 ~ 1123) wrote in the Rubaiyat:

"Ah, fill the cup: what boots it repeat (drink and be merry) / How time is slipping underneath our feet: / Unborn tomorrow and dead yesterday, / Why fret about them if today be sweet!" (Translation by Edward Fitzgerald, 1809 ~ 1883)

3. An awareness of our own end also spurs us to ask the big questions, such as "Why are we here?" Not that we'll arrive at conclusive answers, but at least it will open the gateway to a life filled with mystery and exploration.
4. It also forces us to think about what is important and reminds us to get our house in order. That is, the time to think about securing our family's future by freeing them from debt is now, while we are still alive and can do something about it.
5. It's a great way to kick start our goals, for if you slack off too much, it's like having the Grim Reaper kick you in the butt, saying, "If you want to get something done, you'd better do it now because I'm close behind!"
6. Focusing on our own death is an opportunity to become painfully aware that everyone around us is also dying. We don't know how long they will be with us. So, the time to apologize, make amends, express our affection, offer our respect and forgiveness is now. Our tears are no consolation to the dead. It is the living that needs our kindness.
7. Awareness of our own death also opens our eyes to the pain others are feeling. Do you want to become a volunteer? What greater service can you offer than helping others cope with their death? You can make a valuable contribution by volunteering in a hospice or MTC (Make Today Count) Support Group (support group for patients with terminal illnesses).

Here is a useful exercise you can perform: What if you knew you would die in three months? What would you do differently? Well, start doing that today, for the time remaining is briefer than a wisp of smoke.

The subject of death may appear to be morbid or unnecessarily negative to some. But it need not be when viewed in the right light. For as Elizabeth Arden (1878 ~ 1966) wrote, "Death not merely ends life, it also bestows upon it a silent completeness,..." If that needs further explanation, here is Morris B. Abram (1918 ~ 2000) to fill in the details, "A painting on a canvas of infinite size, worked on eternally, would be without focus, meaning and probably without beauty. A painting, as life, needs limits." So, as we go about creating our lives, it is like creating a storybook, and like all other books, our story cannot go on forever because it needs to end with a point.

A. Sachs wrote, "Death is more universal than life; everyone dies but not everyone lives." Why doesn't everyone live? Because they are trying to vanquish the fear of death, instead of use it in a positive way. We want to be aware of our mortality; nevertheless, our focus should remain on life.

For like everything else, it's a matter of balance. That is, we don't want to ignore death, but neither do we want to be obsessed with it.

48

Overcoming Laziness

Am I going to hell because I'm lazy?

Do you know what the seven deadly sins are? According to the Catholic Church, they are: pride, sloth, gluttony, anger, envy, avarice, and lust. Sloth? What's that? No, it's not a monkey that hangs upside-down from a tree. It's just another word for laziness, idleness, indolence, sluggishness, or acedia. Do you know what a deadly sin is? (They're also known as capital or mortal sins.) Well, if you're guilty of committing one and die before receiving absolution from a priest, the consequence is deadly; mainly, everlasting damnation! Now, perhaps, you can understand my concern. You see, I'm lazy, and what some may call old, so I may be condemned to hell at any moment!

I know what you're thinking, if I'm so worried about it, why don't I change my religion? I'm afraid that's not much help. You see, all religions, as well as the ancient philosophers, condemn laziness. I even tried Zoroastrianism, but one of their demons, named Bushyasp, is actually laziness incarnate. Imagine having a demon named after you! Don't ask me to try Confucianism either. I already looked into it. Confucius believed that earthquakes and natural disasters were warnings from above that the "son of Heaven" (Emperor) was too lazy! Even benign Buddhism condemns laziness as one of the Five Mental Hazards (the other four are sensual desire, ill will, worry, and doubt).

What's all the fuss about?

I don't have any problem when God commands, "Thou shalt not kill" or "Thou shalt not steal," but, "Thou shalt not be lazy" seems a bit harsh. However, after thinking about it, I came to realize that when we're lazy, we are guilty of killing. Killing time. Which is another way of saying killing life. For idling away time is not living; it's lingering. Don't we grow old more through laziness, than through age? If we want to be lazy, why not just die? Perhaps that is what the Hindus mean by their proverb, "It is better to sit down than to stand, it is better to lie down than to sit, but death is the best of all."

We're not only guilty of killing when we're lazy. We're also guilty of stealing. For as the scripture of Zoroastrianism states: "If one does not perform duty to one whom the duty is due, one becomes a thief of the duty." (Avesta, Videvidad 4.1) Goofing off at work? If so, we're stealing from the boss! The concept that laziness is stealing is an important one. For we have roles to play and people are counting on us to perform our duties. When we fail to do so, we are stealing from them. Yet, it's not only others that we steal from. For each time we decide to do nothing, we are shortchanging ourselves, stealing from ourselves, robbing our own potential.

Did you ever take a lot of trouble to select a gift only to find the recipient didn't appreciate it? Ingratitude or thanklessness is not a trait to be admired. Imagine being God and dispensing the greatest gift of all, life. What if that gift wasn't savored, wasn't used, wasn't glorified, wasn't appreciated? Is laziness a sign of the appreciation of life, or is it an indication of our ingratitude? This is a question my wife asked herself when she saw me slumped over the computer keyboard. Gently shaking me, she roused me from my slumber and asked, "Are you being lazy again?" I awoke with a startle and quickly explained, "No, I'm not being lazy. I was just meditating on the vice of sloth."

During my meditation, another point arose in my consciousness. Mainly, whenever we are lazy, we are losing momentum or heading downhill. In either event, not a very good place to be. Before laziness becomes a habit, we should heed the following warning, "How long will you lie there sluggard? When will you get up from your sleep? A little sleep, a little slumber, a little folding of the hands to rest and poverty will come on you like a bandit and scarcity like an armed man." (Proverbs 6:9-11) By now you may agree with me that laziness is not as trivial as I first imagined. How can we tell when we're being lazy? All we have to do is ask ourselves, "Is there a better way for me to use my time?"

Slaying the dragon of sloth

If I were to say, "I am lazy," it implies that I cannot change. But that is not true. Of course, I can change. So, the correct statement is, "I am a person that sometimes engages in lazy behavior." The first step in slaying the dragon of sloth, then, is to monitor our thoughts and correct them when necessary. Once we stop saying "I am lazy," we are preparing ourselves to slay the dragon before it devours us.

We often avoid tasks because we find them overwhelming. We can solve this problem by taking baby steps, or as Mark Twain explains, "The secret of getting ahead is getting started. The secret of getting started is breaking your complex overwhelming tasks into small manageable tasks, and then starting on the first one."

Remember, we are never lazy when it comes to the things we want to do; so, it is not a matter of a lack of energy, but a lack of motivation. Therefore, to overcome laziness, we need to master motivation. If our reason to act is great enough, we will have the will to act. We need to think. Think of the reasons why we want to act. Think of and focus on the benefits we will gain by acting.

Frequently reflecting on the person we can and want to be can help motivate us to act.

When the CEO of a large company was asked how many people worked in his office, he replied, "About half." The other half were goofing off. How come? It's about motivation or the reason for acting. For many people, the sole purpose of work is to make money. In other words, their job is merely the means to an end (money) and not an end it itself. And why do they want money? Possessions. A new car, stereo, or home. If their only reason for working is to make money, they will soon resent their job for "interfering" with the pleasure of spending money and enjoying their possessions.

Our job is not a chore we need to do to get paid, but an opportunity for us to learn, contribute, grow, make friends, solve problems, overcome obstacles, and experience victories. When we see it for the opportunity it is, we will find our job exciting and have little time for idleness. Opportunities abound. They follow us. Whether we're at home, in the office, or strolling in a park. Opportunities are the rays of sunshine that banish the shadows of laziness. No wonder lazy people appear to be asleep. They are in a stupor, unaware of the opportunities hovering around them. Busy people are aware, awake, and alive. So, instead of worrying whether I'll go to hell after I die, I think I'll start focusing on whether I'll live before I die.

49

Overcoming Loneliness

We are all sentenced to solitary confinement

Loneliness is both pervasive and unavoidable. Temporarily experiencing loneliness after the death of a spouse or child is normal. But after loneliness is triggered by an event, care must be taken to immediately begin on the road to recovery, even if it takes a year or longer to heal completely. If we do not aggressively attack it, there is the danger of getting mired in chronic loneliness. It is at such a time that we sentence ourselves to solitary confinement.

Some of the many events that can trigger loneliness are: retirement, job loss, a career setback, death of a loved one, a sudden disability or serious illness, substance abuse, discrimination, estrangement, imprisonment, shyness, children leaving home, relocation, divorce or the end of a relationship, obesity, isolation, rejection caused by one's sexuality, mental or physical abuse, real or imagined rejection, homelessness, and the absence of spiritual, religious or life-affirming beliefs.

Loneliness-triggering events for children include, criticism, corporal punishment, sexual abuse, their parent's divorce, not enough time spent with working parents, transfer to a new school, and schoolyard bullying. Even the rich, famous, and powerful can suffer from loneliness. For example, they may be suspicious of the motivation of everyone in their lives. After all, it may be difficult to distinguish between sincere friends and 'groupies' that merely wish to share the limelight.

How should we respond when a loneliness-triggering event occurs in our lives? There are only two things we can do. We can allow the event to seize control over our lives, or we can remain in control. If we choose to succumb to loneliness and wallow in self-pity, our negative attitude will drive others away, isolating us, and thereby beginning the dangerous downward spiral that can lead to chronic loneliness. On the other hand, we can recognize that loneliness is a natural and inevitable experience that will defeat some and strengthen others. We can choose to join those who decide to overcome their suffering. Why not become a victor instead of a victim?

Overcoming loneliness: Here are some steps you can take to release yourself from the prison of loneliness.

Be your own best friend. Learn to like yourself. I don't mean that you should become egotistical, but just that you should feel good about yourself. Follow your conscience and you will be proud of yourself and happy to be in your own company. As Wayne Dyer wrote, "You cannot be lonely if you like the person you're alone with." Jean-Paul Sartre reversed the same idea when he wrote, "If you are lonely when you are alone, you are in bad company." So, if you are bad company, improve yourself until you are a pleasure to be around! If low self-esteem is holding you back, don't just whine, pick up a good book on the subject and apply its principles. If you are troubled by psychological pain you experienced in your childhood (criticism, rejection, ridicule, etc.), you can also learn how to heal your 'wounded child.' There are many excellent books on the subject.

Help others. Loneliness drains one's energy. Lonely people may just sit around hoping to be noticed. Instead of focusing on themselves and experiencing their own pain, why don't they look outward and notice the pain of others? Think of all the lonely people in hospitals, for instance. Why stay at home and mope when we can visit hospital patients and relieve their loneliness? If we were to do so, wouldn't our loneliness disappear? Isn't it true that if we wish to have a friend, we must be a friend? Experience the insight of Dag Hammarskjold and you'll be on the road to recovery. What was his insight? Here's what he said: "What makes loneliness an anguish is not that I have no one to share my burden, but this: I have only my own burden to bear."

Accept responsibility. Stop blaming and start taking responsibility for the choices you make. It's time to make the right choices. You deserve to be happy. So, take the steps that will pull you out of the gutter of loneliness. Blame is self-defeating. Responsibility is self-actualizing. Live by the precept, "If it is to be, it is up to me."

Journaling. Need someone to talk to? Talk to yourself in a journal. Keeping a journal is cathartic. It will help purge yourself of negativity. Ask yourself questions and sit in silence until you get answers. Record the answers and apply them to your life. Example questions are: What would it be like not to be lonely? How would I act differently? What can I do to change my attitude and behavior? When will I accept responsibility for my own actions? When will I begin to take the steps I know I should take? What can I do now to begin overcoming my loneliness? Journaling is a valuable tool in regaining control over your life. There are several great books on the subject, look into it.

Join groups. You can meet many people at church groups, clubs, associations, volunteer groups, and adult education classes. While there, don't look for friends, but look for opportunities to befriend others; don't look for someone to heal your loneliness, but look for chances to heal the loneliness of others. For it is in giving that we receive.

Plan in advance. When you know in advance that you will be alone, prepare by renting a hilarious video, borrowing an inspiring biography from the library, or catching up on chores you've been meaning to do.

Focus on the positive. If you don't have any friends, look in the mirror, and what do you see? A smile or a frown? If we walk around with a chip on our shoulder, we drive people away. Conversely, if we are polite and friendly, we attract others to us. If you wish to attract birds, scatter bread crumbs, if you wish to attract friends, scatter seeds of love.

Exercise. Loneliness is a state of passivity. To erase it you need to be active. Get involved in an exercise program. Exercise will make you feel better by improving your health, lifting your spirits, and boosting your confidence. And while doing so, you may make new friends.

50

Overcoming Problems

Every problem leads to one of two choices

Some say life is a struggle. If it is, every problem we face leads us to one of two choices. Either we choose to be victorious or we choose to be a victim. Either we choose to be responsible for the life we create or we shirk our responsibility by blaming others for our failures and unhappiness.

Those who choose to be victorious don't find life to be a struggle. They find it to be exhilarating. They don't encounter PROBLEMS; they merely face THINGS THEY WISH TO CHANGE. When they find something blocking their way, they look for a way to get around it or to overcome it. In other words, they look for, and find, solutions. On the other hand, those who choose to be victims are experts at looking for excuses. They almost delight in finding others to blame for their self-inflicted misery. Let's take a look at two real-life examples.

Carl is in his fifties and claims he wishes to recover from a long string of failures. To this end, he enrolled in a college course to update his skills. One day, when the instructor was writing on the blackboard, he shouted from the back of the room, "Write larger! I can't read what you're writing."

Carl was miffed when the instructor ignored his pleas. A few weeks later, he complained to his classmates, "I'm afraid I'll have to drop out of this course. I have bad eyes and our teacher writes too small. How can I take notes and learn the material? Our instructor doesn't seem to care about my 'disability'."

"Why don't you come to class early so you can get a seat in the front of the room?" suggested a classmate. "Because the bus in my area runs only once an hour. If I took the earlier bus, I would arrive much too early." replied Carl. "Get a pair of glasses." another classmate advised. "I have a pair," said Carl, "but they are not very helpful." Exasperated, another classmate asked, "Well then, why don't you get a pair of opera glasses?" Carl had an answer for that too: "I can't afford opera glasses. I can barely afford to pay the bus fare to get here."

Carl had an answer for every question. Although he could never find solutions for whatever was troubling him, he was proficient in finding excuses for his inaction. He was convinced he had certain 'disabilities' that warranted special treatment. The world should conform to his 'special needs,' he reasoned.

Kyle Maynard is an entirely different breed. Born with stumps in the place of arms and legs, he believed it was his responsibility to adapt to the world rather than demanding the world change for him. The challenges that Kyle has to face make Carl's pleas for special treatment embarrassing at best and laughable at worse.

Despite the enormous obstacles facing Kyle, his lack of arms and legs did not prevent him from learning how to write and type. Neither did it prevent him from becoming a defensive lineman on a football team, a university student, and the top wrestler in the state of Georgia. Though still a university student, you can add to his list of accomplishments author, world traveler, and motivational speaker.

"No Excuses" is the title of Kyle's book (Regnery Publishing, Inc., 2005), and it points out the difference between him and Carl. Kyle realizes that making excuses holds us back while assuming responsibility moves us forward. He understands that responsibility is empowering, and the more of it we take on, the more we will be, do, and have what we want.

Problems, difficulties, challenges, or whatever we choose to call them, shouldn't stop our progress. Rather, they should cause us to ask the following three questions. 1. What do I want from life now? 2. What is preventing me from getting what I want? 3. What am I going to do about it?

The answer to the first question introduces purpose, direction, and meaning to our lives, for when we know what we want to be, do, and have, we have goals to achieve, mountains to climb, and a reason for being.

The answer to the second question is the first step in finding a solution. After all, we cannot solve a problem until we admit that we have one.

The answer to the final question comes in the form of steps we can take to defeat our difficulty. It is a road map, an action plan that, as long as we follow it, will take us where we wish to go.

Those who choose to be victims can usually answer the first question because even they know what they want most of the time. However, they blind themselves to the truth when it comes to the second question. For instead of looking for solutions, they doggedly search for excuses. They blame anything or anyone else for their problems. They refuse to get involved in finding a solution because they are, after all, victims. Their answer to the question, "What am I going to do about it?" is "I am going to do nothing. I'm going to stay put. Even though I'm unhappy where I am, I'm not going to change. I prefer to have the world change, and I refuse to do anything until it does."

If there is something in your life that you wish to change, but are finding it difficult to do so, you may find it helpful to understand the five steps of change.

In the first step of making a change, we will feel AMBIVALENT. That is, we will both want to and not want to change at the same time. That is perfectly natural. You see, although we WANT TO improve our lives, we DON'T WANT TO experience the immediate, though temporary, discomfort that usually accompanies making a change. So, when you find yourself hesitant, don't get discouraged. Rather, understand the cause of your hesitancy, focus on the benefits that change will bring, and force yourself to take the right steps.

You begin the second step of change when you answer the third question (What am I going to do about it?). For the second step of change is one of preparation. In this stage you outline the steps you need to take to get you where you want to go.

The third step is implementation. That is, you carry out your plan by taking the necessary steps.

The fourth step is broadly called maintenance. You check your progress and make corrections when needed. Reworded, you make sure you stay on course and are headed for your target.

The fifth step or stage of change isn't experienced by everyone, but is important to understand. It is the step called relapse. You may suddenly find that, despite your initial progress, you have slipped back to your previous state. Like step one, relapse is a natural event. It is to be expected. Although not everyone experiences it, many people, if not most, do. So when it happens, just pick yourself up, brush yourself off, and say, "I'm not going to get discouraged and give up now! I refuse to choose to be a victim! I choose to be victorious, so I'm getting back to the program of change and regaining control over my life!"

51

Overcoming Procrastination

Procrastination is the grave in which opportunity is buried

Imagine being in a graveyard, examining a gravestone. Despite being covered with moss, you can read the inscription. It says, "Procrastination is the grave where your dreams, aspirations, and hopes lie." Is that where you want you dreams to end up? Buried? Aborted? Each time we put off doing what we wish to accomplish, each time we procrastinate, we bury our dreams. Or, as Victor Kiam said, "Procrastination is opportunity's natural assassin."

Although it's not something we like to do, occasionally we should reflect on our mortality. We need to remember that we will die. For when we do so, it will be clear that the time to realize our dreams, the time to act, is now, not some vague date in the future. Why do we complain that life is too short and then throw away pieces of it by procrastinating? Why have we been so slow to learn? After all, 2,000 years ago, Emperor Nero's adviser, Seneca the Younger taught, "We all sorely complain of the shortness of time, and yet have much more than we know what to do with. Our lives are either spent in doing nothing at all, or in doing nothing to the purpose, or in doing nothing that we ought to do. We are always complaining that our days are few, and acting as though there would be no end of them."

Why do we procrastinate? One reason is an incorrect way of viewing life, a false perspective. We not only create the words we use, but later allow those words to create our perspective. Take the word "work," for example. Its connotation is negative. We don't think of it as a gift, but as punishment from God (Genesis 3:17). It is something unpleasant and to be avoided. Therefore, we put off doing it.

Although we may talk about "going to work," can you imagine Picasso, Michelangelo, or Mozart saying the same thing? They may have spoken about creating art, but never of working. How can doing what you love be considered work? If we realize that we are artists and the work we do is the medium we use to create our masterpiece, we too can come to love what we do.

Another major reason for procrastination is the feeling of being overwhelmed. The task just seems to be too much to handle. But if we remember that a 1,000 mile trek begins with a single step, we will have the courage to begin. So, regardless how big your dream may be, if you break it down into small tasks, you will be able to accomplish it, one step at a time.

Fear of failure is another reason why people procrastinate. For instance, suppose someone dreams of writing a book. As long as they plan to write it "someday" in the future, they can brag about it. But what if they start and finish the project, and there are no buyers? Ugh! They'll be a failure! Or will they be? How can they be a failure if they learn something from their mistake? Don't let fear stop you, for as David J. Schwartz writes, "To fight fear, act. To increase fear -- wait, put it off, postpone."

Human nature also plays a role in procrastination, for we naturally avoid pain and are drawn to pleasure. So if we view our chore as a PAIN in the neck and watching TV as a pleasure, we will likely postpone the chore and watch TV instead. But before we do so, it would be wise to consider what Edwin C. Bliss wrote: "... FCC Chairman Newton Minow referred to television as a 'vast wasteland'... and it conjures up... a landscape littered with countless ruins of unfulfilled plans, aborted ventures, unrealized dreams... of the viewers, who try to select the least tedious of several mediocre shows instead of turning the set off and doing something."

Let's not be like most people who sit around waiting for their ship to come in, only to discover it is a hardship. For as Abraham Lincoln said, "Things may come to those who wait, but only the things left by those who hustle." If you still have problems with getting things done NOW, you may want to consider joining Procrastinators Anonymous (they've been around for years, but have never gotten around to having a meeting).

52

Overcoming Temptation

Most of us know what we wish to be and do. Yet, we are occasionally tugged away from our path by temptation. It comes to us in many forms. We may be enticed to gossip instead of working, watch TV instead of cleaning the house, or hang out in the pub with friends, instead of studying for an exam. The surest way to be nothing is to do nothing. Conversely, the surest way to be something is to do something.

Temptation is a fork in the road. When it beckons, it says, "Come follow me and I will make you less than what you can be." But when we decline to follow it, we make ourselves more than what we are; we make ourselves stronger. For as Ralph Waldo Emerson wrote, "We gain the strength of the temptation we resist." So, temptation is a blessing, for it is an opportunity to grow stronger and practice integrity by being true to ourselves.

Overcoming temptation

Overcoming temptation is possible and worthwhile. When you make it a habit, you are liberating yourself from enslavement by negative behavior. The whole world opens up. You find you can soar like an eagle and accomplish your dreams. So, how do we overcome temptation? The following techniques will help.

1. How can we improve if we are in the habit of acting without thinking? The first step in overcoming any bad habit is to become aware of our thoughts. In this case, when temptation

strikes, we need to be aware of it. Once we are aware, we can consciously decide on what action to take. Many of us, however, are not in the habit of being aware of our thoughts. We act as robots, allowing our thoughts to control our actions. But when we are aware of our thoughts and control them, we are free to create the life we want to live. The best way to learn to be aware of your thoughts is to practice meditation. That is, just sit still and consciously observe the thoughts flowing through your mind. Observe them without being judgmental or reacting to them. Just be an observer. If you regularly set aside 20 minutes to practice, you will become skillful at being aware of your thoughts throughout the day.

2. The next time you are aware of the presence of temptation, ask yourself, "What's in it for me?" If I succumb, how will I benefit? If I cave in, will I later regret it? The mere act of reflecting on the pros and cons will weaken temptation's grip on you. Once you realize the lure of temptation is harmful, dismiss the thought and get back to what you were doing. The less we focus on a particular thought, the weaker it becomes. So, when temptation comes knocking, be aware of it; question it; dismiss it, and get on with life. Another way to put it is: instead of fighting your thoughts, merely observe them. For example, if you find yourself craving a cigarette, you could say to yourself, "That's interesting, I'm suddenly craving a cigarette. I wonder what triggered that desire. Is it stress, my body's desire for a "fix" of nicotine, the time of day, or something I just heard or saw?" Observing and analyzing your thoughts will help neutralize their power over you.

3. Another approach is to immediately replace the negative enticing thought or behavior with a positive thought or

action. In a word, think of or do something else, something useful. Craving a cigarette? Get up and do some sit-ups or drink some water instead!

4. Temptation gains its power by linking itself with an emotion. You need to remove the emotional hook. For example, instead of thinking about the temporary pleasure temptation is dangling before you, reflect on the pain you will later experience should you give in to it. That extra piece of cake may be pleasurable now, but how will you feel after gaining weight and entrenching a bad habit?
5. Avoid the trap of promising yourself to act correctly later. Instead of saying, "I know that extra piece of cake isn't good for me, but it's just for today. Tomorrow, I will cut out cake altogether." If you give in to your craving, you are doing more than eating a piece of cake. You are also strengthening a bad habit, which will become even more difficult to break tomorrow.
6. Respect the adage, "An idle brain is the devil's workshop." In other words, keep busy. Idle time is an opening for temptation. I'm not suggesting that you should never relax. Not at all. But relaxation or recreation is the reward we give ourselves AFTER we perform our duties. They are not meant to be a substitute for work or responsibilities.
7. Are our jobs and obligations exciting or boring? The answer to that question depends on ourselves. It depends on our attitude and view of life. If we choose to see our responsibilities as thrilling opportunities, how can we be tempted to stray? But should we persist in viewing our duties as tedious, we are inviting temptation to call on us. So, a change of attitude may be called for.
8. A change in our way of thinking may also be necessary. We may have some false beliefs that need to be changed. You

have false beliefs if you find yourself saying things like, "I can't resist temptation. I was born this way and can't change. It's too late to change." When such thoughts occur, immediately challenge them. For example, it should be obvious the statement that you can't resist temptation is untrue. Of course you can resist it. You may not want to because you are focusing on immediate gratification instead of long-term benefits. Or you may simply find it difficult (not impossible) to resist because you have already established a bad habit. By questioning your assumptions you will have the opportunity to correct the errors in your thinking and make changes for the better. It may not be easy, but you can do it. Remember, it's not easy to get to work on time every day, but you do, don't you?

9. Common sense suggests that if we wish to overcome temptation, we need to avoid situations that force us to confront it. If you're trying to give up smoking, does it make sense to spend the coffee break with your friend who is a smoker? Wouldn't it be wiser to hang out with nonsmokers?
10. What is it that you want to be and do? What are your goals? If you make it a habit to focus on your aspirations for a few minutes every day, you will find it much easier to resist temptation's call. Focus on what you want to be instead of what you want to have (which is a few minutes of temporary pleasure).

I'll close by paraphrasing the early Sufi Master, Abdullah Ansari (1006-1089): If thou canst walk on water, thou art no better than a straw. If thou canst fly in the air, thou art no better than a fly. But if thou canst resist temptation, thou canst conquer the universe.

53

Overcoming Your Past

There is a plethora of information on NLP on the Internet and scores of books on the subject. If you wish to explore the subject further, a great place to start is with Harry Alder and Beryl Heather's *"NLP IN 21 DAYS, A Complete Introduction and Training Program,"* Piatkus (press), 1999.

NLP has given birth to many effective techniques for change. NLP practitioners refer to these techniques or tools as applications. I will introduce one such application for the sake of Abigail and others finding it difficult to let go of the past. I call this application "Overwriting Your Past."

If you have computer experience, you may have tried to save a new file with the same name as an older file. When trying to do so, you will usually be warned that if you continue, the new file will overwrite the old one. That is, the new file will replace the old one, and the old one will be erased from the computer's memory.

Isn't our brain a computer? Aren't our memories files? Why not overwrite painful memories (files)? To practice the "Overwriting Your Past" application, we first have to place ourselves in the alpha state (a state of relaxation). The instructions on how to do so appeared in the previous issue, but for the benefit of those who missed it, I am repeating them here (steps 1 ~ 3).

1. Find a place where you will not be disturbed. Shake out body tension. Be seated and get as comfortable as possible. Close your eyes and take three deep breaths.
2. Slowly inhale and imagine the number three flashing three times as you slowly breathe out. Repeat this for number two (see it flashing three times as you slowly exhale). Next, repeat this for number one.
3. Imagine sitting before a black curtain with a bowl of white numbers (1 ~ 10) at your side. Reach into the bowl, take out number one, stick it onto the curtain, and then remove it. Repeat this with number two, continuing until you have done all ten numbers.

   Steps 1 ~ 3 remove your thoughts from the cares of the day, help you enter a relaxed state (alpha), and prepare your mind to focus on the "Overwriting Your Past" exercise. At this point you will be prepared for the next step.
4. In your mind's eye or imagination, relive the painful memory. Turn it into a movie. Watch it from beginning to end.
5. Now that it is a movie, play it in reverse. Try it in slow motion and fast rewind.
6. Now play it in fast-forward. Notice how it takes on the almost comical appearance of an old silent film.
7. Add music to your movie and change the scene to a carnival or Mardi Gras atmosphere. Watch it in fast-forward and reverse.
8. Add props. Do you remember those funny plastic eyeglasses with huge eyebrows and a huge nose? Place one on the

antagonist in your movie (in Abigail's case, she would see her father wearing these ridiculous eyeglasses as he belittles her). Dress the antagonist in an outrageous costume (perhaps as a clown). Watch this new version of your movie in forward and reverse.

Tinker with the speed if you wish.

9. Add character voices to your movie. Change the lips of your antagonist to the bill of a duck and give him or her a Donald or Daffy Duck voice. Watch your new movie in forward and reverse. Give the villain of your movie any other absurd voice you can think of. Watch and enjoy!

As you practice the "Overwriting Your Past" application, you will find that your original painful experience will slowly be transformed into something funny. If not funny, something so ridiculous that it is powerless to harm you.

Practice this application for 30 minutes a day for as long as needed, which should be no longer than two or three weeks. Thirty minutes a day for 21 days works out to just ten and a half hours. That's less than half a day's work to end a problem that plagued Abigail for more than 50 years! How powerful is this application? If all you do is read about it, it is powerless to help. But if you follow the steps and apply it to your life, like other NLP tools, it is life transformational.

Do you, like Abigail, have a disturbing memory that haunts you and holds you back from enjoying the limitless freedom and happiness you deserve? If so, why not rewrite your life? Why not overwrite your past? Why not set yourself free? After all, all you have to lose is the chain that is holding you back. Do you want to learn 100 more NLP applications? If so, check out the "NLP Toolbox" at: http://www.nlptoolbox.com.

Despite the usefulness and power of the "Overwrite Your Past" application, it is not always the best approach for everyone. After all, even in conventional and integrative medicine, patients respond differently to the same form of treatment. So, the more weapons in your arsenal or arrows in your quiver, the greater your likelihood of success. With that aim in mind, here are more techniques to cleanse you from the toxicity of holding a grudge. I'll divide the techniques into three groups: Compassionate, Psychological, and Spiritual.

1. Compassionate

a) The Deathbed Visualization. Buddha asked, if you realize everyone will die, how can you treat them cruelly? With that thought in mind, Buddhist monks practice a 'Deathbed Visualization.' That is, if they are the object of cruelty, they imagine the perpetrator on his or her deathbed. Such an image evokes compassion rather than anger. Don't those who are drowning flail about wildly? They don't wish to drown their rescuers; their wild behavior is caused by their desperate attempts to survive. So it is with those who are cruel to us. They are on their deathbed. Confused, they are drowning in the sea of life, wildly flailing about, wildly striking out, desperately trying to survive in the only way they know how. With this realization, how can we be angry with them? How can we refuse to forgive them?

2. Psychological

a) Understanding the Cause of Pain. A kicked dog bites not because it is vicious, but because it is defending itself. Similarly, most of the people who act cruelly do so not because they are mean-spirited, but because, like the dog, they have been injured in the past and remain in emotional pain. The short "Story of Bobby" will help you understand this point; Whenever we have to bear the brunt of a cruel remark, it helps to ask ourselves, "What could have happened to make that person act that way?" By reminding ourselves that cruelty flows from pain, it becomes far easier to forgive.

b) People Just Do Their Best under the Circumstances. We are not perfect. Sometimes we act stupidly and hurt others. Not because we're bad, but because we do the best we can at any particular time. If we cannot control our own behavior, how can we become offended by someone who is guilty of the same offense? Here's a good habit to get into: whenever someone offends you, in your mind state the offense and add the phrase "just like me." For example, if someone is upsetting you because they are hogging the conversation and not giving you a chance to speak, rather than getting upset, say to yourself, "They are hogging the conversation and not giving others a chance to speak... just like me." You see, the plain truth is what we don't like about others is what we don't like about ourselves. But because we don't like to admit our faults (even if it is only to ourself), we project them on others. Take advantage of this fact by using the world as a mirror for self-improvement. In other words, when you don't like the behavior of others, repeat the "...just like me." sentence in your mind, and in your heart thank them for pointing out an area that you can improve on.

c) Understand the Cause of Your Pain Is Not the External World, but Your Internal World. Most of us are somewhat fragmented. It is almost like having multiple personalities. There is the person we REALLY are, the person we THINK we are, and the person we PRETEND to be. Also, for a detailed look at our fragmented, many selves and how to heal or integrate them, see: *THE MISSING PIECE, Solving the Puzzle of Self*, by Claudia Black, Ph.D. and Leslie Drozd,

Ph.D., Ballantine Books, 1995. By learning how to forgive ourselves, we will become well equipped to forgive others.

d) Hypnosis. Another tool employed by NLP practitioners is hypnosis. If you're looking for a good, FREE, software package that will hypnotize you, give you hypnotic suggestions (that you can edit or create), and wake you up, look no further than Virtual Hypnotist. You can learn all about it and download it at: You can use self-hypnosis to improve yourself in all areas of life. But before embarking on an auto-hypnosis odyssey, be sure to study the basics. One book that will give you a solid and comprehensive view of hypnosis is "*SELF-HYPNOSIS for the Life You Want*" by Charles E. Henderson, Ph.D., Biocentrix, 2003. You can visit Dr. Henderson's site (and order his book) at http://www.bcx.net/hypnosis/aboutceh.html.

3. Spiritual

a) Acceptance. The main teaching of Buddhism and Taoism is acceptance. That is, we accept what cannot be changed. No complaints, no whining, no struggle. On the contrary, we embrace what is and "go with the flow." If we unconditionally accept everyone we deal with, there will be no need for forgiveness. What's more, when we accept life, rather than fight against it, we will not experience frustration and bitterness.

b) Transcendence. The spiritual path is one of transcendence. That is, we seek to become more than we are, greater than we are, nobler than we are. What better way to uplift ourselves and change desperation into inspiration than by forgiveness? For as Edwin Hubbel Chapin (1814 ~ 1880) wrote, "Never does the human soul appear so strong and noble as when it forgoes revenge and dares to forgive an injury." Consider also the following words found in Hindu scripture (the Mahabharata), "Forgiveness subdues all in this world; what is there that forgiveness cannot achieve? What can a wicked person do unto him who carries the sabre (saber) of forgiveness in his hand? Fire falling on the grassless ground is extinguished of itself. An unforgiving individual defiles himself with many enormities. Righteousness is the one highest good; and forgiveness is the one supreme peace; knowledge is one supreme contentment; and benevolence, one sole happiness."